Focus on the 90%
One simple tool to change the way you view your life.

by Darci Lang

Distributed by

X-L Enterprises Inc.
P.O. Box 32077, Regina, SK S4N 6E0
Ph: (306) 569-1354   Fax: (306) 569-1356
E-mail: info@darcilang.com
www.darcilang.com

Cover design: brent pylot
Cover illustration: brent pylot
Photo of Darci Lang: Mark Greschner

Library and Archives Canada Cataloguing in Publication

Lang, Darci, 1969-
    Focus on the 90%: one simple tool to change the way you view your life / Darci Lang.

ISBN 978-0-9783157-0-2

    1. Attitude   change.   2.   Optimism.   3.   Self-actualization (Psychology)
I. Title.

BF637.S4L3535 2007   158.1   C2007-901540-9

Focus on the 90%

Focus on the 90%

Acknowledgements

Thank you:

To my husband Darren — I am your greatest fan. Together forever, and this day.

To the most amazing children in the world, Jayda and John – I love you and I am so proud to be your Mom.

To my "many extended families" and friends who continue to love and support me.

To my editorial team, Jean, Jeanne, David, Cari and Brandie, for helping me to sort the 90%s from the 10%s and see which are which!

To all the wonderful audience members I have met, and continue to meet — you touch my life.

And above all, thank you God — thanks for every day I wake healthy with fingers able to type and a heart eager to share my message with those who are ready to hear it. Thanks for the words you give me to say, and for inspiring me to do what I do. Thank you for helping me to stay focused on the 90%s in my world.

Focus on the 90%

Contents

Focus on the 90%

Introduction

I have learned many lessons about the importance of focusing on the positive 90%s in life. I have also learned many, I wish I would have — I should have lessons as well. Choosing to see the positive 90% in yourself is not an easy task. Choosing to see the positives in others is not either.

I'd like to tell you a short story that is very near and dear to my heart. This story is important to me because it not only shows the focusing on the 90%

idea in action, but the event itself really helped me to understand this idea and just how powerful it can be.

Let me tell you about my mother-in-law, Dorothy. My husband Darren's Dad passed away when he was eight years old leaving "Dottie" to raise her three boys. Darren is the baby boy of a Roman Catholic mother.

Let's just say that when I first met my mother-in-law, we did not see eye-to-eye. She had a very strong personality and was immediately "over-mothering" me. I locked my magnifying glass on the 10% of Dottie that rubbed me the wrong way and that is all I could see. I was sure that I was not her first choice as a mate for her baby either. I was broke and had never been to church a day in my life. Not exactly what she was hoping for. Though she was always very nice to me, it just did not start out well. The first three years were kind of rocky. Darren and I bought a house close to her, but I didn't respect her the way I should have.

Ten years ago my beloved Grandmother, Nan, passed away. I remember sitting at her funeral thinking, I wish I would have ... I should have. My grandmother was one of the most important people in my childhood and I did not tell her enough how much I loved her and how much I appreciated all she did for me. I remember that quiet two hour drive home from the funeral with Darren. I remember sitting in that passenger seat thinking, I never want to do that again. I never want to sit at the funeral of another person, wishing I would have and I should have. I decided to make a mental list of who else's funeral I would be likely to sit at and say that. The first person to pop into my mind was Dottie.

I thought about it for most of that ride and then I said to Darren, "You know what. When we get into the city, drop me off at your Mom's. I want to talk to her." He looked at me and said in a worried voice, "Why?". I told him not to worry I just wanted to clear the air.

When Dottie opened the door and asked how the funeral was, I told her the story. I told her how I thought of her on the way home and did not ever want to say, I wish I would have and I should have with her. I asked her to forgive me and ... that loving Christian woman did.

We started with a clean slate and I made a choice to start seeing her positive 90%s. Sure, she still over-mothered me and popped into our house whenever she felt like it, but there were so many positives about her.

She shared great stories about the joys and hardships of being the oldest of 13 siblings on a dairy farm.

She talked about her late husband John and how much she loved and missed him. She talked about when he got sick and how hard it was to care for a dying husband. I started to really admire this woman. She had a grade 8 education when John died, and while raising her three boys and working full time, she earned a University degree. She loved to shop and travel and had over 200 pairs of shoes.

I am a very conservative dresser while she loved anything red and anything with sequins on it. We had opposite tastes in dress. She bought me red clothing that I never dare wear. My closet contains more red clothing than I can count! She didn't like my hair down. She thought I should wear it up. "It is much prettier that way", she often told me.

Every time we go on a road trip for a speaking engagement she calls and leaves a long message on our phone telling us the same thing every time. "*If you see something up ahead on the highway slow down until you know what it is, many lives were saved on the farm by slowing down*". I could recite the message word for word I had heard it so many times. It drove me crazy!

I love this woman. I know we still get on each others nerves but we accept and love each other. Our bond is the wonderful man she raised, our Darren. I often think about how without her, I wouldn't have him.

Dottie was not raised to be a hugger. I was. So I always left her with a hug and told her I loved her. She always hugged back and said the same.

Five years ago Dottie at 64 years of age passed away from a sudden brain aneurism. We never got to say good bye.

The first thing that came to my mind was Thank God. Thank God I made a choice and moved my magnifying glass. Thank God I told her I loved her the last time I saw her. No regrets.

The things I miss the most are her pop in visits , my red clothing and I dearly miss that message on my answering machine as I pack up to leave for a road trip.

I delivered a portion of the family eulogy at her funeral. It was by far the toughest "gig" of my life. Four hundred and fifty people packed the church on that sunny July day. Bright pink flowers lined that big altar. The same altar where I was baptized and married. Dottie's beloved Sweet Adeline's sang "I will raise you up on the last day" as her casket was wheeled up to the altar. It was one of the most emotional days of my life. I wondered how I would keep it together and deliver the eulogy.

It was my turn to speak. I walked to the altar. I wore the most amazing red suit. I wore a sequin shirt underneath. I wore my hair up. I looked like a hooker! But Dottie would have loved it!

I stood in front of that group of 450 people and I said:

"Let's each live our life like Dottie did. Let's live our life so that 450 people attend our funeral and miss us as much as we will miss her.

Let's go and live our lives so that we never say ... I wish I would have ... I should have ... Let's tell the people we love that we do love them every day so that you will never wish you had.

I will never regret the time I had with this amazing woman. I will never forget how she shaped the woman I am today. She is a true example to all of us that life is short and is so precious.

Leave this church today with an attitude that you will never regret. You will say sorry, you will forgive and you will love. Let's live each day like it may be our last."

I will always be grateful I moved my magnifying glass off the 10% of Dottie that bothered me or rubbed me the wrong way and onto the 90% that was wonderful, loving and supportive. This simple shift in perspective gave me one of the most precious relationships I have ever had ... and I could have missed it. It lets me look back on our time together with no regrets, just fond memories.

So how can focusing on the 90% positive work for you. Lets take a closer look at the 90% idea and discuss how it can help you live a happier and more connected life.

The positive 90% idea

My hope is that this book will offer you one single idea that will help you to live a happier life. Not nineteen ways or six ideas. *Just one – Focus on the 90% that is positive in your life, rather than the 10% that is not.* This one tool is enough to change your life.

Focusing on the positive 90% has changed my life. I believe we hold a sort of mental magnifying glass out in front of us in our lives and we can choose to do two things with that magnifying glass. We can choose to focus it on the positive 90%s in our lives that work, or we can **choose** to focus it on the negative 10%s that don't work. What we focus on determines how we live our lives.

Everyone's got their problems. And I find too often, people get pre-occupied with what they don't like about themselves, or their spouse or their jobs. Dwelling on these 10%s can be exhausting and only serves to distract you from the 90% that you love about yourself and the significant people in your life. Why isn't 90% good enough? When you were in school, if you got 90% on an exam I'll bet you were pretty happy (or at least 90% of you were). We are not perfect, our spouse isn't perfect, nor are our children, friends, coworkers or job. We discover true peace of mind and a lot happier life when we learn to accept this and start focusing on the 90% that works.

In this book I will challenge you to ask yourself whether you hold your magnifying glass on the positive 90% or the 10% when it comes to all of the areas of your life. I will cover five areas in this book. I ask you whether you focus on the 90% or the 10% when it comes to yourself, your family, the people around you, your job and your clients.

What do you focus on when it comes to yourself? No one is perfect. Are you trying too hard to be? Do you tend to focus on your 10% negatives and not your own 90% positives? Let's make life easier for ourselves. With stress and depression at an all time high; how can we learn to focus more on what is good in our lives?

What you focus on with your family? Many people tend to give 90% at work and 10% at home. In this book we will talk about having something left for the people we love. Whatever family represents to you, we have a choice as to how we treat our family at the end of the day.

What about the people around us? Most would agree that a negative person can bring down a group. So what do we do with those "10%ers" around us? Since we can only control ourselves, not others, how can we learn to exist successfully among people who are unhappy?

What do you focus on within your job? Have you ever met anyone who complains about their job? In this chapter we will talk about what happens when we take a negative attitude to our workplaces. What happens to us and the people who have to work with us? We will talk about the 'ripple effect" of a negative attitude at work. How can we learn to find the positive 90% in our job? And if we can't find anything positive, is it time to move on? What options do we have?

What about our clients? We all have accountability to our businesses or organizations to give our clients the best possible service. This includes those clients who just seem to be unhappy no matter what service level we provide to them. We put unrealistic expectations on ourselves and our staff to think that "the customer is always right". 10% of the time the customer is cranky no matter what we might do for them.

– • –

We read motivational books and we see speakers share their messages on staying positive. We hear great information that we know we should apply to our life but often it just seems too overwhelming.

Too many ideas and just not enough time. That's why I wanted to give you one idea in this book. Focusing on the positive 90% not on the negative 10%. It is one simple message that has made a world of difference in my life.

One thing I have discovered is that life is really short. As I write this book I am 37 years old. It feels like only yesterday I was 18 years old (with the same hairdo!). I have already lived one third of my life. I want to spend the next two thirds of my life happy and living each day … ok, 90% of my days ... to the fullest. I don't want to be at the end my life saying I wish I would have ... I should have.

We really do have a choice about the attitude we have towards ourselves, our families, others and our jobs. Let your choice be a positive 90% one.

Focus on the 90%

Lets talk about you.

Not everyone is going to like you. At least 10% won't. But the happier you are with yourself the less likely their opinion will have an affect on you. People who seem to be unhappy in their job and with others; they seem to be unhappy with themselves too.

How we feel about ourselves relates to how we interact with others. It starts with us. The saying,

"You can't love others until you love yourself" is very true.

As children we are taught that focusing on the positive 90%s of ourselves is bragging. Saying a simple thank you to someone when they say they like what you are wearing is hard for many people. Some people tell me that they grew up in families that taught them to down play their positives. Perhaps we call that a form of humility.

I used to do a workshop in my presentations where I would ask people to share a 90% positive about themselves in front of the group. I stopped doing that because so many people would tell me they were not comfortable doing that ... or worse, they had nothing to say.

I am not perfect. I don't want to be. The women that I know in my life who are trying to be perfect are missing out on life along the way. I am only 90%, in all respects. It is a complete transformation to get me from au naturel to the way you see me on this book!

But I have learned to accept my 10%s and move on. We have many 90%s. Honor yourself and your positive attributes.

– • –

My sister-in-law told me what a woman said at their annual block party BBQ. One of her neighbors asked: "Are you related to Darci Lang, the speaker?" When my sister-in-law responded, "Yes", her neighbor said, "She must be perfect.". My sister-in-law said to me, "Don't worry. I told her for fifteen minutes that you weren't!"

My initial thought was, "I'm glad she said that because no one is perfect and I don't want anyone walking around thinking that."

It wasn't until later that I thought ... Hey, wait a minute, that wasn't really a compliment was it? Ha ha! (And I still love my sister-in-law!)

– • –

The Cracked Pot (A tale from India)

A water bearer in India had two large pots, each hung on one end of a pole which he carried across his neck. One of the pots had a crack in it, and while the other pot was perfect and always delivered a full portion of water at the end of the long walk from the stream to the master's house, the cracked pot arrived only half full.

For a full two years this went on daily, with the bearer delivering only one and a half pots full of water to his master's house. Of course, the perfect pot was proud of its accomplishments, perfect to the end for which it was made. But the poor cracked pot was ashamed of its own imperfection, and miserable that it was able to accomplish only half of what it had been made to do.

After two years of what it perceived to be a bitter failure, it spoke to the water bearer one day by the stream. "I am ashamed of myself, and I want to apologize to you." "Why?" asked the bearer. "What are you ashamed of?" "I have been able, for these past two years, to deliver only half my load because this crack in my side causes water to leak out all the way back to your master's house. Because of my flaws, you have to do all of this work, and you don't get full value from your efforts," the pot said.

The water bearer said to the pot, "Did you ever notice the beautiful flowers along the path? Did you notice that there were flowers only on your side of the path, but not on the other pot's side? That's because I have always known about your flaw, and I took advantage of it. I planted flower seeds on your side of the path, and every day while we walk back from the stream, you've watered them. For two years I have been able to pick these beautiful flowers to decorate the house."

Each of us has our unique flaws. We are all cracked pots. It is our flaws that make us unique and special.

– • –

What makes you special? Create a 90% list for yourself. List all of your positive attributes.

Give it to your friends and loved ones and ask them to tell you why you are special. When you are having a 10% day … read your 90% list and the comments you have gathered.

– • –

Let's start at the beginning.

Where does how we feel about ourselves start? Most would say our childhood and I would have to agree. Many people tell me that their childhood is what has shaped them and how they feel about themselves. Very few people I have met say they had the "perfect childhood". How we see our childhood is how we perceive it. If we view it through our 10% magnifying glass we only see the unhappiness ... if we learn ... (key word "**learn**") … to move our magnifying glass to the "90%s" we start to see the positives.

I was born in 1969 in small town Saskatchewan, Canada. My parents Beverley and John did not stay together and through the years have been married three times each. Eleven of us children have come together in those six marriages.

For many years I viewed my childhood through my 10% magnifying glass. I spent many years, "blaming" my childhood for my life.

Thirteen years ago at 24 years of age I had a "Quarter-Life Crisis" (It's great now because I don't have to have a Mid-Life Crisis. I'm done!)

While the tuxedo company I was working at was going under, I felt I was going under too. I was broke, unhealthy and very unhappy. I was feeling very sorry for myself. I remember during that time I called my Dad. I told him I was sitting in my rented dirt basement house, like the one he and I had lived in. I told him that it was interesting irony that life puts you right back where you started. I also told him that I was blaming him for the mess I was in. I told him, if it wasn't for the childhood I'd had, I would be better able to deal with my life.

My "tough love" Dad said to me over the phone, "You know what Darc; you can only blame your parents until you are 18 years old. You made that mess you are living in … now go clean it up".

I was not very happy with my Dad at the time for that reaction. But I am now. I think if it was not for that call, I would still be living in that dirt basement house blaming everyone else for my life. I had no one left to blame but … me. I decided he was right; I needed to clean up my life.

I went and got some counseling. I had met so many people in my life who were unhappy because of their past. Some people carry those issues around like luggage for the rest of their lives. I've met people in their 50s who were still blaming their parents for their lives.

I also went to the library (since I couldn't afford to buy anything) and looked in the self-help section. I found a book called "Attitude your most Priceless Possession" by Elwood Chapman. I picked it up and opened a page. As Oprah would say it was my "Light Bulb Moment". The page said: "we hold a magnifying glass out in front of us and we can choose what we focus it on".

That book started to change my perspective on how I viewed my job and the people around me. Most importantly it started to change how I viewed my past and myself personally.

I realized right there in that library that yes ... 10% of my childhood was not positive ... but 90% was. I had spent so many years playing the movie of my childhood with my magnifying glass stuck on the 10%s that I couldn't see the positives. And there were so many.

For example: when you are raised by that many parents, do you see how many grandparents that added up to? Christmas was amazing; I just went from house to house and "raked it in". I had six different houses to visit!

So many people were positive in my life.

My grandparents — Nan and Pop — taught me unconditional love. My summer holidays at their house playing with my cousins are the happiest memories of my childhood.

My Dad taught me how to hug and tell people that you love them. His motto was to never leave anyone you love without telling them you love them first. He taught me to be a communicator. He taught me perseverance, a strong work ethic and how to be an entrepreneur. He also taught me ... girls can do anything they want to do.

My Mom Beverley taught me forgiveness. Life is too short to carry around burdens that do not bless your life, or the lives of others. My Mom is a survivor in every sense of the word and she taught me strength. She is an example to me of living life full.

My step-Mom Sandy raised me like her own daughter and taught me so many things. Most of all she taught me to see the good in others and that people need to live their life the way that is best for them. She raised me through my 10% teenage years and still loves me! After years of being raised by Dad as a grease monkey in the garage, she taught me about hair and make-up … thank goodness!

Each step parent, aunt and uncle that touched my life loved me and taught me a bit of them. I am the oldest child from the original "union" of parents so I am older than my siblings. Each brother and sister taught me what it is like to love a child. It has shaped the mother I am today.

Sure, the 10%s are still there … they always will be. The past can not be changed. I have made a choice to forgive people and move on. I made a choice to focus on the 90%s.

I had an audience member come up one time and hand me a small card. It read: "**Forgiveness is giving up the hope that the past can ever be**

different". But the future can be different when you change your focus to the 90%.

My friend Jean said, "You made a choice to put the FUN back into dysfunctional".

– • –

What are the positives of your childhood? What are your happiest memories? Even if your childhood was a tragic one, there must be one or two 90%s ...

– • –

The Catholic Experience

I have made a lot of mistakes in my life. Things I wished I wouldn't have ... things I should have. Parts of my early adult life I wish I could just erase, but they too have shaped who I am today.

I had always dated the same guy, different hairdo. Then I met my husband Darren. I became many things when I met Darren: first, I became the luckiest woman in the world. I also became two other things — a Roman Catholic and a Saskatchewan Roughrider Football Fan. Both of which require a lot of praying and forgiveness! Ha ha!

I had never been to church a day in my life. Especially a Catholic Church! Darren and I wanted to start our relationship on a positive note so we came together with our list of what we were looking for in a mate and at the top of Darren's list was, "She needs to be a Roman Catholic". He was everything on my list so I decided I would give this religion thing a try. He was worth it.

I remember the first time I attended church with Darren. I expected to see a 200-year-old priest bent over the altar reading Latin bible verses for three or four hours. Instead, I was greeted by a handsome middle-aged priest with a huge smile who looked at me, looked at Darren and said, "Where did you pick her up?" Father Joe Balzer, "Balzer" as Darren called him, was one of the nicest men I've ever met. Church was a wonderful eye-opener. I saw families with five and six children, all from the same mother and father ... what a concept!!

For eight months Darren and I attended RCIA classes, the Rite of Christian Initiation for Adults. These classes would prepare me for my baptism that Easter. Father Joe Balzer, Deacon Joe Lang and their team taught me many things in that time. I took away many great life lessons during that time and the greatest thing I took away was the ability to **forgive others and yourself as you have been forgiven**. Most importantly, forgive yourself too.

I remember standing at that altar 12 years ago on Easter weekend with my family and friends in the pews. Father Balzer leaned over and whispered in my ear, "Hey Darc, this is your chance to wash away all of your sins." I whispered back with a smile, "Do you think we have that kind of time?"

– • –

The serenity prayer

God grant me the serenity to accept the things I cannot change
The courage to change the things I can
And the wisdom to know the difference.

– • –

How much is enough?

We have talked about focusing on the positive 90% of your past. Now let's talk about the present. I think one of the most stressful things we do to ourselves ... especially my generation ... is that we are on the endless pursuit of the 10%. We are consumed with what we do not have rather than what we do have. I feel blessed to come from very little material wealth. It taught me to appreciate all that I have.

My house is not perfect. I live in middle class suburbia in a house as old as I am. I love our house. Darren and I have painted every wall; I have sewn every curtain. We saved and scrimped to buy this house, our dream home back then. We have carried two beautiful newborns through the door and raised our babies in our amazing tree-lined back yard. We have the greatest neighbors ... something you don't usually get to pick! We have toys strewn all over the yard and Jayda and John's crafts taped up all over the kitchen. My fridge door is overflowing with pictures of family members and friends.

We have family pictures displayed all over our house, and the challenge is to arrange them so the visiting family is up front!! Everyone who visits says, "This is a house you can really live in! " (I choose to take that as a compliment!)

We have many friends and family who say, "Why don't you move into someplace bigger/newer/nicer"? I always answer "Why"? To me the endless pursuit of more wastes the time I could be living. I can't keep clean the size of house that I already have! Don't get me wrong when I visit my friends in their shiny new houses I do feel pangs sometimes.

I honestly think that being happy with what you have is one of the secrets to happiness. I intentionally live well below my means. I would rather work less, eat organic food, take a winter holiday and buy shoes!! Why do I need a bigger house? Sure I like nice things but I am not always willing to pay the price, literally or figuratively.

What happens if we don't learn to focus on the 90%s?

Bob, Candace and their two small boys lived in our neighborhood years ago. Candace was a happy, beautiful woman and a wonderful mother who loved being a stay-at-home Mom. Bob was more reserved but friendly enough. One thing that really stood out about Bob was that he was a perfectionist. Their vehicles were spotlessly clean. Their house, their clothes, their yard ... all perfect. He would cut the edge of his grass with scissors! Many times I drove by, watching his boys play as he worked, and I hoped he took the time to play with them too.

Now don't get me wrong, I am a "doer"! I never sit still but I know the times I need to stop and just "be".

I noticed a "For Sale" sign on Bob and Candace's lawn. I found out they had bought a brand new house in a more affluent neighborhood. I slipped a card in the mailbox wishing them well and telling them we would miss them. We lost touch.

A couple of years later I was in the grocery store shopping without my children. This is what I call in my world …"an outing". As I turned the corner to head down an aisle I spotted someone familiar, it was Candace. I stopped in my tracks as I got closer to her. Candace was still as beautiful as ever, but I could tell something was wrong.

We were the only two in the aisle and we met half way. She looked up and we made eye contact. I didn't have to ask how she was … I could see it in her eyes. I walked closer and asked her, "Candace is everything all right?" She started crying, standing in the middle of the grocery store aisle crying her eyes out. Now I am crying too, and I don't even know why we are crying. We are now hugging too in the middle of the aisle.

Out of the corner of my eye, I can see some men coming up the aisle. They see us crying and hugging and make one big 90 degree turn and head the other way! Whatever our problem was, they were not coming near us! I imagine they were a few tins short of a full load of groceries when they went home that day!

As we regained our composure she asked me if I had time to talk. She said, "Darci. This is so weird. I was thinking about you this week. I wanted to call you and share a story with you". She dug out Kleenex and juice boxes from her shopping cart. We sat right on the bottom shelf in the middle of that grocery aisle and talked.

Candace started by saying: "I have a story for your presentation about what happens if you keep focusing on the 10%s instead of the 90%s. You must have noticed Bob's personality, how obsessive he is. The way he is with the yard is the way he is with everything else in his life. Nothing is ever good enough for Bob. That is why we bought the new house, new cars and new furniture. Stuff we couldn't really afford. I was really happy in our old house but he wanted to "keep up" with the Jones'.

Bob manages 15 people in his job and 14 of his employees love him. One doesn't. All he talks about is how he can make that one person happy. His customers love him but he obsesses over the 10% that he doesn't serve perfectly. Then Darci, when Bob comes home at the end of the day, we are never good enough. The house is never cleaned to his perfect standards. Now the boys are in school he expects them to excel in everything. Nothing makes him happy. We have so many positive 90%s in our lives but he can not see them! He is so wrapped up in his obsessive behavior that he is missing all the great things.

Well Darci, last year Bob did it to himself. I knew it was just a matter of time before it all got to him and sure enough, it happened. He started to get worse and worse. He started sleeping a lot and snapping at us all the time. He started to call in sick to work and watch television all day. Not like Bob at all. Finally his boss told him he needed to take a break for a while. When he was off, he just started slipping away. I begged him to get help but he was too proud. He finally went to see a counselor who diagnosed him with depression and suggested he try some medication. Bob was too proud to take a pill. No man in his family would ever do that.

It's a big mess. I have lost my husband and the boys have lost their Dad. It has been so hard on all of us. I have told Bob if he doesn't do something to make himself feel better, I am going to leave.

The reason I wanted to call you Darci is because Bob's story is a living example of what happens when you only focus on 10%s. When your magnifying glass can only see what is not right or good in your life, you miss out on all the positive 90%s along the way. Something the counselor told Bob was if he had only gotten the help he needed earlier … when he felt himself slipping … he would not be in the state he is now.

He said something that really made me think of you, Darci. He told Bob, 'If you feel overwhelmed, you are'."

I know so many people are overwhelmed and it is affecting their lives. I do believe if we get the help we need earlier the 10%s do not grow to be our 90%s.

– • –

Ask yourself if you are overwhelmed. What can you do about it? Do you need counseling? Do you need help?

– • –

34

Triple Espresso

I don't drink coffee very often anymore, but once or twice a week I love to have a coffee mid-afternoon. I'm like Jerry Seinfeld; I get my coffee on the outside. The caffeine really affects me! I am usually up painting a room after the kids have gone to bed!

Recently I arrived at my local coffee shop and walked passed the only other vehicle in the parking lot, a big truck with a construction company logo on the side. I got in line inside behind a big burly tough looking guy whose appearance matched his truck. He was dressed in construction boots and coveralls, his neck and hands tanned from working outside. I could just feel the tension coming off him. In a tired voice he ordered a coffee with three espresso shots in it. I thought I had heard him wrong. Obviously the woman behind the counter did too as she asked him to repeat it. He explained to her that he wanted her to put the espresso into the coffee to make it stronger. She joked with him saying "Stronger is not the word". He just looked blankly at her as if to say, "Just get me my coffee".

I stood there thinking if I drank that coffee I could paint the entire house!!

He paid for his coffee, walked to the area where the cream was, put cream in his coffee. He stood at the counter and drank the entire cup in about ten seconds. He put his cup down and walked out.

All I could think was ... wow! What is going on in this guy's life that he needs this kind of caffeine injection? From inside the coffee shop I could see him approach his truck. He could not see me but I watched him get in, sit down and put his head down on his steering wheel. I watched his shoulders shake and realized that he was crying. After a few moments he lifted his head and looked around to be sure no one had seen him. He wiped his eyes with the back of his hand and drove away.

I watched that tough guy and I thought of Bob. This guy has to go back to his construction site and pretend like everything is ok. He was clearly overwhelmed. I prayed that he would seek the help he needed to get through. I also prayed that someone at work might notice his sadness and offer a listening ear.

– • –

Getting help takes courage. Don't be too proud or too tough to ask for what you need.

– • –

Three times vent rule

Here is my deal about stress. Whether it is stress from the past, future or the present, consider the three times vent rule.

I have a huge family as a result of my childhood. I am now blessed with a circle of really amazing friends. My deal with them is this: I have a "three times vent" rule. The rule is that I will lovingly listen to their problems, concerns, challenges, stresses … three times. Everyone needs to vent. (Especially us women). My Dad taught me it is healthy to vent your stresses; it is not healthy to keep them bottled up. Three times friends or family can come to my table and I will honor them and whatever their stress is. I will hug them, cry with them, feed them and booze them. I will not offer advice or give them a seminar (which is hard for me!). I will just listen and be there for them.

BUT … if they come a fourth time, I am going to ask them this: What are you going to do about it now?

I will ask them to lay their problem/stress out on the table and make an action plan to deal with it. "Lay that sucker out" is the way I generally put it. I will challenge them to ask themselves: do they need help dealing with this problem? Do they need to have a talk with the person? Do they need marriage counseling? A parenting class? A new job? Is it something from the past they can not solve? It isn't healthy for us to carry around the same stress for days, weeks or even years, and not take any action to solve it!

Venting turns into plain old complaining when we vent the same thing over and over and over again.

I speak from the experience of carrying around many of my own stresses for years until I finally had to say … Enough! So one by one … and it took me months … I laid those "suckers" out and I dealt with them. Besides, I can't get away with venting to my friends more than three times either!

– • –

What suckers do you need to lay out? Lay them out one by one and do not try to tackle too many at once. You can only deal with one at a time. Go easy on yourself and ask for help if you need it.

– • –

How do you feel?

A sucker I had to lay out was my energy level. I needed to keep up my energy to deliver full-day presentations and still be as energetic for the people I love waiting at home for me at the end of the day.

So I laid it out. Since I was complaining more than three times about being tired all the time, I started to do some reading and research on health and feeling better. For years now I have been on the endless pursuit of what I can do to feel optimum. So I have something left for me and my family at the end of the day.   Feeling good is everything. Everything stems from how you feel.

I remember listening to a Zig Ziglar tape in which he said if you had a million dollar race horse, would you keep it up half the night giving it booze, cigarettes and junk food?   Of course not! So why wouldn't we take care of ourselves like we would that horse.

When you feel good you have a better attitude, you are more patient, loving and understanding towards yourself, and towards your family.   Taking care of my health and eating properly has been the key to maintaining a positive attitude. If I feel good…I act better. Period.

I am a border line fanatic about this now. I can't believe the energy and mental clarity I have gained. Even on an interrupted sleep night.   90% of time in my house we eat my way, 10% of the time we eat Darren's way. (Sounds like a fair ratio to me). Coming from a farm background Darren thinks each meal has to have meat in it; vegetables have to have cream sauce and two meals a day should end in pie.   So I give in at least 10% of time.   As Darren reminds me, "A man can not live on organic vegetarian food alone". On the weekends I do chow down and live a little!

I take handfuls of seaweed, omega oils and assorted vitamins and supplements. I eat organic food; I drink my water and green tea and indulge in my beloved coffee a couple of times a week. I have to tell you I feel amazing. So does my family, eating this way. I would like to die when I am 111 years old. The only way that will happen is if I take care of myself today.

My Mom Beverley is a breast cancer survivor and she has a poster on her office wall that reads ... "If you think money is everything ... you have never been sick".

Quit cleaning on Saturdays!

As I entered motherhood my stresses grew. I wanted to be the perfect mother and wife. I was having such a hard time keeping up everything that life threw at me. I was working, cleaning, packing, nursing, doing and doing and I was never ahead! (Maybe you can relate to this?)

Two babies in 22 months made it a busy household. (When you are my age you gotta crank em out!!) I can live in a certain amount of disorder but then I get a bit ... goofy when the mess builds and builds. I tended to take that out a lot on Darren. I would complain constantly about the mess. I didn't want to clean all day Saturday; I wanted to be with my family. Even though I was doing a good job of "focusing on the positive 90%" and not trying to be overwhelmed, I was really starting to lose it! Then one day after I was ranting about the mess AGAIN to Darren he said, "I think you have complained about this more than three times ... maybe it's time to lay that sucker out". He thinks he is funny!

So I did. I got a cleaning service. I feel very blessed to have the money to have this service come in. All I have to say is ... what took me so long? They come and they ... "shovel" the house out. It is so great! Debbie, one of the women who has cleaned for us in the past, said, "I love cleaning your house. I feel such results when I leave!" (I appreciate her sense of humor!)

I have a magnet on my fridge that says: Do Less ... Be More. It reminds me of what is really important.

– • –

Pick up the phone book right now and call a cleaning service. Sacrifice a meal out, a new shirt, or something ... to get this done. Oh and you perfectionists, accept that it will not be the job you can do ... and don't clean before they come!

– • –

One huge sucker that many of my audience members say they need to lay out is more time with their families. Balance comes up over and over. Guilt is something parents deal with all the time. How can we learn to have more balance and less guilt? Let's talk about our families now.

Focus on the 90%

Your family.

— • —

So many people are dealing with guilt and balance issues. I say one of the greatest ways to deal with these challenges is to give the best of you when you are with your family. When we go home and give what is left over ... we feel the guilt. Have something left for the people you are doing this for in the first place.

Why do we give 90% to our jobs and everyone else and only 10% to our families?

– ● –

The Door Knob Theory

I have had the honor of speaking and training for thirteen years. I have consistently arrived at my engagements friendly, full of energy and excited to be there. Even on the times when I haven't always been healthy and had to deliver programs sick as a dog, on little sleep, and in some cases when raising our children, on NO sleep! ... I never let the client or the audiences know, and I always gave the best of me.

I would do all this for my client but I would come home and sometimes I would not be the same woman. I would not be the same friendly, full of energy person to my family that I was to my audience. Why not?

Let me tell you about my family. My Darren is one of the nicest people you could ever meet. He is kind, considerate and a wonderful husband and

46

father. He has many 90% qualities but he does have some 10%s too (as do I!) In our house Darren is considered by me and most of the people around us, "the third child". Every day has to hold some fun and adventure for Darren. He can not just "sit around". Darren grew up on a Saskatchewan farm with his two older brothers. On the farm Darren would catch wild frogs and play for hours with his new found pets.

While golfing one Saturday last summer Darren discovered the same kind of frogs living in the water beside the golf course. Much to my horror, Darren brought his first set of frogs home for our children to play with ... or should I say, for "all of them" to play with!

This summer he took it up a notch. He built in our back yard a home for the frogs to live in. The frog "sanctuary" as he calls it - is built with fiberglass walls and a chicken wire-type top that the neighborhood children can peer in to see our new ... pets. It looks like a see-through compost. Darren dug up a part of their "dirt" from their water source and built a small swimming pool so the frogs can swim in their lovely new habitat. We live in the city and we have ... wild frogs! Jayda and John ... and Darren ... play with the frogs, and when they have all "escaped" ... they get new frogs. They put them in a pail in our mini van and bring them to their new home.

Our daughter Jayda, much like her Dad, must go on an adventure every day. Like her Mom she never sits still and never stops talking! She is an amazing child and I love to just watch her play. She has the greatest laugh and she loves to create, craft and play with small animals, stuffed or real! She loves frogs, stuffed and real, and her friends think she is so lucky to have so many pets. She names most of her frogs "sweetie" and all the green ones are named "Saskatchewan Roughrider."

Our boy John is named after my Dad and Grandfather and Darren's late father. He is a very special little boy. I always say, how couldn't he be with a man like his Dad to model after? He is quieter than Jayda, but he too loves to go and "do something fun". John loves his Mom (which of course, I love too!) and his superheroes. Since a very young age he has been fascinated by anything Spiderman or Batman. He will not wear **anything** that does not have a superhero embellished across the front. All of his frogs are named of course, Batman and Spiderman.

When I am away on a summer day speaking, Darren has spent the entire day with our children. Now I am not sure if that conjures up any imagery?

A day with Daddy will start like this: Jayda and John wake up. They are in their pajamas. Darren never changes them out of their pj's. They walk around all day like that. His theory is ... they are going to bed again anyway! I have to buy them pajamas that resemble clothing. Jayda has been known to go to school in her pajamas!

John loves it; he gets to wear his Spiderman pajamas all day! My friends will call and say, "I knew it was Darren's day with the kids. I saw them at the park today and the kids weren't dressed!" People think it's cute ... I beg to differ.

As I mentioned, health is very important to me and I am committed to feeding my family healthy things. But ... when Mom is speaking, guess where they go for lunch? Oh yes ... McDonalds and Dairy Queen for dessert! So by early afternoon my family has been to a couple of parks, and a couple restaurants … all in their pajamas. And now it is time to "go catch frogs".

So when I drive home from my engagements, I am already mad. I spend the entire drive home focusing on the 10%s and thinking about the mess the house … and Jayda and John … are going to be. Rather than taking the time to focus on the positives of my life, I contradict the message I just spent all day sharing with my audience members, and I focus on the 10%.

When I arrive home, things are exactly as I imagined. Things are a complete mess. There is a trail of sand from the sandbox (one that's big enough for Darren to fit in!) into our house. Dirty dishes are all over the counter. Backpacks and muddy shoes are by the door. All the couch cushions are off and they have built a fort in the living room.

I look outside and sure enough, my family is in the yard, having a "frogging" good time. I see Jayda and John in their filthy pajamas with McDonalds and Dairy Queen still on their face. My handsome Darren hasn't showered, shaved or changed his shirt. I head out into the yard. The fun's over … Mommy's Home.

I walk in the yard and I "start". I start complaining about having to come home to a mess. Though I know they will help me clean it up later on, I feel mad because they didn't do it before I got home. And how come I don't have time to "frog" all day! I line everyone up like a drill sergeant and get everyone cleaning up. John says "You're not as fun as Daddy!"

Then I lie in bed at night and I feel bad. I feel guilty. I blew it. I had a few precious hours to spend with my family and what did I do? I spent the time focusing on the 10%s rather than the positive 90%s. Why didn't I play? Why didn't I just take a few extra moments when I walked in that door to show my family a positive wife and mother? Why don't I make more time to go and be someone who catches frogs?

Did you women ever notice that we set the tone for our houses? Did you notice that those first few minutes set the tone for the entire evening? You know the saying… "If Momma Ain't Happy – Ain't nobody happy." It is so true in my house. My mood is the mood of my family.

I read in a parenting book that we should treat our children and our spouse like we treat our best business client. What courtesy would we extend to them that we do not extend at home? I think if we come home at the end of the day with nothing left for our families, they start to resent our jobs too.

I made a choice. I had had enough of feeling bad about how I greeted my family at the end of a long day. I had enough of being the parent that was not the "fun one". I was tired of being the Mom on the blanket on the beach and not in the water. I was tired of being the Mom at the water slides who was not going up and down with her children.

So I laid that sucker out (not Darren, the problem, ha ha). I made a choice. I thought about the fact that if a client called me, no matter what time of day, I would be full of energy for them. Without exception. So how come I could not pull from the same energy place to give my family my energy? Without exception.

I sat the three most important people in my life down and told them that I would be the same woman off stage that I am on stage when I am speaking. I will come home and give the best of me because they deserve it. The accountability piece for them was that they needed to chip in more so I did not feel like the nagging door mat.

So I made a choice. Was it easy? Nope. I start by making sure that my drive home is positive. I spend the entire drive focusing on the positive 90%s rather than the negative 10%s. I thank God for a career I love and can't wait to get out the door and do. A husband who plays with his kids and builds frog "sanctuaries". Two beautiful, healthy children. A warm house, two cars and my health.

I came up with what I call "The Door Knob Theory". The idea is that I will not enter that door unless I am in a positive mind set. I put my Focus on the 90% mini-magnifying glass reminder in my car and one in the inside of the garage door to remind me to be positive. Sometimes I stand in the garage for 15 minutes praying for strength! But it changes me. I walk in now and the mess is not the first thing I see. I see my family with their sun-kissed faces.

I take off my suit jacket and my heels and I head out into the yard with a smile on my face to see how many "Saskatchewan Roughriders" they caught today. I hold the frogs, I sit on the grass and tackle and kiss my kids (and even Darren occasionally!) and I focus on what is positive, my 90%s. I am fully present and there for them. Now the challenge is: who is more fun, Mom or Dad?

I try to make all areas fun, grocery shopping and running in the aisles, loud '80s music as we clean the house and dance around. I didn't know how to be fun. I had to learn that. It helps having a fun husband.

I thank Darren for being the man that he is and for being the kind of father who would have that much fun with his kids. When Darren was building the frog "house" a friend was visiting, and she said, "You are so lucky to have a husband who would do that". She is so right.

Sure we need to clean. There are realities of life. But something happens when you just take a few minutes to let your family know you are happy to see them and you appreciate them.

Go catch some frogs; it's good for the soul.

– • –

Think about how you can make a choice to make a positive impression when you get home at the end of the day. Implement the Door Knob theory in your house and do not enter that door until you are positive first.

– • –

If I can't do anything right... I won't do anything at all.

Like many husbands, my Darren needs a lot of positive feedback. I learned this very early in my marriage. Focusing on Darren's 90% is a way to keep his self-esteem (and his housework motivation) high. However I found for the first few years of our marriage that when Darren tried to help me around the house it was never quite … good enough. It wasn't up to my "standard". (Those were the days before children so I actually had a standard.)

He rolls towels and jams them in the linen closet. His idea of making the bed is just pulling up the bed spread, sheets all bunched underneath. Or worse, he doesn't make a bed because … his theory is: we're going to bed again anyway!

I used to do a lot of nagging about this silly 10% stuff when one day Darren said, "You know when you make me feel like I can't do anything right, I don't want to do anything at all".

I decided to practice my own message. I would focus on the positive 90% instead of the negative 10%. So what if you have to pick a dried bit of dried food off a washed dish … it is still washed. Rolled up towels are still clean so I stopped refolding them. And I've finally recognized that maybe he is right … making beds everyday is a bit of a waste of time.

I still slip sometimes and nag about something not being good enough but when I do, Darren says with a sweet smile (and a touch of sarcasm) "10%".

I thank him for everything he does. Every time he unloads the dishwasher or takes out the garbage, I genuinely thank him. I recognized that everything he does contributes to us working together successfully. When I started to do this, something miraculous started to happen: he started to do more.

I know I have a role to play in Darren's self-esteem and motivation. Nagging him does not make him, or me, feel good. That is not the wife I wanted to be. Darren is not perfect but neither am I. He has his fair share of 10%s that bug and annoy me but he would tell you ... and I would have to agree ... I am not always easy to live with some days either. **I find the more I feel better about myself the less I find fault in him.**

– • –

Create a 90% list of your spouse/partner and share it with them. When you find yourself focusing on their

10%s, take out your list and read it. It will remind you of all their 90%s.

– • –

Build them up.

I know I play a very major role in my children's self-esteem as well. Not always focusing on the 10% with them is vital.

When I had children I got a chance to see if the idea of focusing on the positive 90% would help my parenting. When they were learning to walk and talk, the parenting books said to encourage them as much as possible. Every time they said a word or stepped a wobbly step, I gave them a ton of positive feedback to encourage them to do more.

As they grew into toddlers, I made sure I took the time to find the positives in this exciting and changing time. There were many challenging days when I thought I would climb the walls, but I made sure that in the midst of it all, I took the time to tell them I loved them, I am proud of them and their accomplishments. I am not a perfect mother and I have made and I am still making mistakes as I go along. No matter how the day has gone, and some days are 10%s! I make sure I take the time to lie in my children's beds with them at night, and each day to tell them, no matter what, that I love them. I tell them even if we had a rough day that I still love them.

I have met so many people who suffer from low self-esteem. So many who did not hear any positive reinforcement while they were growing up, that I wanted to make sure my children knew how important they were. I tell them how much I love being their Mom.

I am surrounded by a circle of friends and family who are wonderful mothers and I have learned so much from them.

My children are little. I know, "little people ... little problems." People say to me, "Wait until they are teenagers!" Parents say, "Come and talk to me when your Jayda and John are teenagers. We'll see how damn happy you are then!" Ha ha ... perhaps I will write a book in those years and let you know how "Focusing on the positive 90%" is working !

John

I don't think it's ever too late. I don't care if your children are 2 years old, 12, 22 or 42; they need to hear positive comments. It is never too late to tell them.

A young man named John emailed me one morning, and his email read:

"Hello Darci, my name is John. This morning I woke up and there was this small magnifying glass — "Focusing on the 90%" — sitting on the kitchen table. My Mom was at your presentation last night and she taped a note onto your magnifying glass and it said, "John, I was at a presentation last night for work and the woman talking gave us this magnifying glass to take home. She told us it was never too late to tell your children you love them. So John I want you to know ... I love you and I am very proud of you."

John then went on to write. *"Thank you for doing that Darci as I am 18 years old and my Mom has never told me that before."*

Margaret

I told the story about eighteen-year-old John at a huge industry conference. Margaret sat in the front row.

I received an email from her the next day:

"Darci my name is Margaret and I was in the front row yesterday. Two things you said hit me hard. The first thing was you reminded me I have a role to play in my son's self-esteem. My son has suffered from low self-esteem his whole life. The second thing was … I sat there thinking that my son is 28 years old and I have never once told him I love him and I am proud of him. I knew sitting there I needed to do that.

So after your presentation I drove right to his apartment and when he opened the door I gave him a big hug and said, "I love you". I could tell he was quite shocked. He pulled away from my hug and asked me," Mom – are you dying or something?"

Ha ha …

– • –

Do you need to drive to someone's house and deliver a hug?

– • –

Tell her ya love her.

I shared my message one morning with a group of graying men. That morning I would talk about the importance of focusing on the 90% within their own job, with their staff and with their clients. I closed the day with a very strong message that they needed to go home and focus on the 90% there too. It is not okay to go home and not have something left for the people that they love and who love and support them.

I challenged them to be the leaders at home that they are in their very successful businesses. What if at the end of the day they walked in their houses and gave their spouses and children the same respect, time and appreciation they gave their jobs? Many of these men in the audience were heading down the road to retirement. Who would they go home to at the end of their work life? What investment have they made in the people they will spend the rest of their life with? I knew they all knew what I was sharing but my challenge was are they doing it?

An audience member named Frank stood up in the audience and said:

"Darci I will take a lot away from here today. I have two great teenage boys. I spend a lot of time tellin 'em what they should be doing better with their life. I need to tell 'em I am proud of 'em. I am goin' to do that.

I have a great wife and I don't tell her I love her. In fact I often tell her "When I stop loving ya, I'll let ya know!" But seriously, I am gonna go home today and tell her I love her and thank her for all she has put up with. I may even stop at the gift shop here at the hotel and buy her a little somethin'.

But Darci, if I go home today after this three day conference and I start bein' nice to my wife, she's gonna think I was at this conference cheatin' on her!

Well Frank … it's all in the timing!!!

– • –

Do you need to stop at the gift shop too or just tell someone you love them?

– • –

Our wonderful priest, Father Bill, shared this story in his sermon at church last week.

The Trouble Tree.

The carpenter I had just hired to help me restore an old farmhouse had just finished a rough first day o the job. A flat tire made him loose an hour of work, his electric saw quit and now his ancient pickup truck refused to start.

While I drove him home, he sat in stony silence. On arriving he invited me in to meet his family. As we walked to toward the front door, he paused briefly at a small tree, touching the tips of the branches with both hands. When opening the door, he underwent an amazing transformation. His tanned face was wreathed in smiles as he hugged his two small children and gave his wife a kiss.

Afterward he walked me to the car. We passed the tree and my curiosity got the better of me. I asked him about what I had seen him do earlier.

"Oh, that's my trouble tree," he replied. "I know I can't help having troubles on the job, but one thing's for sure, troubles don't belong in the house with my wife and children. So I just hang them up on the tree every night and when I come home. Then I in the morning I pick them again."

"Funny thing is," he smiled, "when I come out in the morning to pick them up, there ain't nearly as many as I remember hanging up the night before".

Choice.

It really is about choices. I have a colleague whose husband works for the oil industry. He is away from home three weeks of the month working, and home with his family for one week. Her children are similar in age to mine and I asked her, "How do you do it?" She said to me, "When Mike is away he is away. When he is home, he is home. When Mike is home for his week with us, he is here for us. He is the best father and husband because he knows the time is short and precious."

Perhaps Mike would rather be with his buddies at Happy Hour when he gets home, but he makes a choice. I am sure it isn't easy some days but his family feels loved and cared for, with less guilt. It is about quality time, not quantity.

Our jobs can impact the man and woman that we are at the end of the day. It is important that we carry the same positive 90% magnifying glass back to our workplaces as well.

Your Job

$-\bullet-$

Have you ever met anyone who complains about their job? We all have at least 10% negative at our job – sometimes it seems like more. When we go to work with our magnifying glass on the 10% of our job the ripple effect is huge. It first affects how we do our job because it is difficult to be enthusiastic about something we don't enjoy.

Then our negative attitude ripples out to our co-workers because it is not easy to work with someone who is complaining all the time. How can we build a "team" with people who drag themselves to work?

Then the ripple effect extends to our customers and the service we provide to them. It is very difficult to provide great service if you have a poor attitude.

When clients call me to speak, to share my 90% message with their staff, they often say that they are having issues with low morale and poor service delivery. I always say the same thing to them... "You must have people in your organization who don't enjoy their job any more". Sure enough, when I speak to the staff ahead of time, it is true. Some have moved their magnifying glass to the 10%.

The ripple effect does not end with the customer service we provide. It is very difficult to provide great customer service to our clients if we do not enjoy what we do. The customers can sense this.

The ripple effect of a negative attitude at work not only affects our work performance, everyone we work with and our clients, it also affects us personally. It *affects our self-esteem because many people tie their self-esteem to their job. Doing something you do not enjoy, or you do not feel is of value, is very hard on you.*

Then the ripple effect extends to our families. When we have a negative attitude at work we tend to bring that home and our family suffers every evening at the dinner table. They hear about how much we dislike what we do.

The ripple effect does not end there. It also affects our children as they watch and listen to us at the end of the day. We teach them that the job that provides for the family is not a place you should go to and enjoy.

– ● –

Janet

I was invited to speak at a Teachers' Professional Development Day. The PDD was two days before the school year started and my job was to pump up the teachers before they started the new school year. I would spend the morning reminding them of the unbelievable importance of their job and how their attitude at work affects everyone they work with, and most importantly, every student they teach.

The first to arrive at the Professional Development Day was a young woman who sat in the front row. No one arrives at a training session first and sits in the front row. Most people who arrive early sit in the back row, and the late people sit up front. Kind of like church.

This enthusiastic woman sat right up front with a great smile the entire time I talked. She sat on the edge of her seat and hung on every word I said. She made copious notes and shared at every workshop opportunity. She was a light in the room! At the break she rushed up to me and said, "You are the greatest speaker I have ever seen!" Then she admitted, "Well, you are the only speaker I have ever seen"! I laughed and asked how she kept herself so positive.

She introduced herself as Janet and explained to me that this was her first year of teaching. In two days she would walk into her first classroom. I went and visited her classroom, all decorated with flowers, bees and happy faces. I wished her well and I said a prayer on the way home that she would keep that enthusiasm for her job.

A year later I was shopping in a retail store with my angels, Jayda and John. The woman helping me seemed very familiar. She was a remarkably capable and enthusiastic sales associate with a great smile, who played peek-a-boo with the kids while I tried clothes on.

When I looked at her nametag, it hit me – it was Janet, the teacher from the Professional Development Day! I said, "Aren't you the teacher I met last year?" She responded "Yes I am! You're the magnifying glass lady ... I knew I recognized you!" I asked her what she was doing working in a retail store. What happened to her teaching career?

She replied, "I taught for a year and I hated it. So I quit", I responded, "Good for you, it takes courage to leave something you don't want to do". She said with a wry smile, "That isn't what my parents had to say about it. They paid for my education."

She went on to explain that she had worked retail during university and thought she could better serve people in a job she enjoyed. Even in her first year she knew teaching was not for her. She said she had seen far too many people in her family stay in jobs that did not make them happy.

As I was leaving with Jayda and John I stopped on the way out, turned around and said, "Janet – Thank you. Thank you for not teaching my children, and their children — with an attitude that shows you don't want to be there— for the next 35 years of your life".

– • –

How do you feel about your job? A good gauge is to ask yourself this: when someone asks you about your job, what do you say? What is the first thing you talk about, the positive 90% or the 10%?

– • –

Richard

Sitting at the front table at one of my presentations was a young man named Richard. He looked unhappy. As I spoke, he gave very little feedback. He just seemed to be in his own world. I shared my message that we need to focus on the 90% that is positive at work and at home. We talked a lot that day about the ripple effect. The effect of arriving at work with our magnifying glass on the 10% and how it effects everyone around us. He left my training day and didn't say goodbye. Just got up and walked out. I prayed he was okay.

The next day I received an email from Richard. Since he seemed so unhappy in the presentation I thought he would be emailing to complain about something. His email read:

Hi Darci. My name is Richard. I was the guy who sat up front yesterday. You might have noticed I didn't want to be there. I didn't want some consultant telling me how to do my job. Minutes into your presentation I knew it would be different. You really struck a chord with me. I sat there listening to you and I realized ... I hate this job. I have worked here for seven years and there is not a day I do not wake up and push the snooze bar 15 times, dreading coming to this place. It is not at all what I wanted to do with my life. I complain at work and at home constantly about what I do. In my selfishness I never realized the impact my attitude must have on my coworkers. Sitting around the staff room listening to me complain about this job must be exhausting for them. I realized what an impact that must have on the service I deliver to my clients. No wonder I never meet my sales goals.

What really hit me Darci was when you spoke about the personal areas of our life. It does affect my self-esteem doing a job I do not enjoy. I have changed. I used to be a nicer person. I have a tremendous wife and two great kids. I can't remember the last time I did not walk through the door tired and pushing my kids to the side. I can't remember a meal I have eaten with my family that I have not spent the entire time complaining about my day.

I went home last night and I told my family I was sorry for doing that all these years. My wife and I sat up half the night talking and we decided we needed to make some changes.

So Darci I wanted to let you know. I walked into my boss's office this morning and I quit my job. And I told him ... it was because of you.

Yikes! That wasn't quite what I had meant, but I emailed Richard back and told him he should be proud of himself. It takes courage to quit. I wished him well in whatever his next venture was to be.

A few emails up from Richards was an email from his boss. The subject line of his email read: *"Thank you"*.

The body of his email read: *"Thank you Darci for helping me to get rid of someone who has been very unhappy in our company for many years"*.

– ● –

Have you ever known anyone who left a job for one that paid less money, in order to be happy? I remember taking a cab ride one time and Bernie the cab driver told me why he left his previous job to drive cab. The stress and pressure of his last job were getting the best of him. He said driving that cab, he didn't make the money he used to but now he had no stress and he had back his health and his marriage.

– • –

We all have a choice about what we focus on at work. We choose the job we have. We can also choose the attitude we bring to our job.

So if your choice is to stay in your job for whatever reason, how can you stay focused on the positive 90%? No job is perfect. The grass is not always greener at another job. The challenge is to find the positives in whatever it is we choose to do for a living.

One way I have found very successful for many of my clients is to stay focused on why you ever wanted this job in the first place. Stay focused on the meaning of the job or the difference you make in the job you do. No matter what the job, you affect someone else by doing what you do. What difference do you make?

– • –

Remembering why you wanted the job in the first place.

I was sitting in a waiting room at a doctor's office. I love waiting in waiting rooms. It is my chance to sit, do nothing and read a magazine. I am always so annoyed when they call my name as I am always half way through a great article!

While I was waiting, a Paratransit van pulled up. I could see out the window into the parking lot and I watched as the driver of this paratransit vehicle jumped out and ran enthusiastically to the side door to help his customer. He helped out an elderly man in his wheelchair. The elderly man was dressed in a sharp three-piece suit and his shoes shined to a perfect polish. He reminded me of my late Grandfather "Pop".

The driver pushed the wheelchair to the disinterested employee behind the counter and announced in a loud voice,"Excuse me. Mr. Wright is here to see you". He turned to Mr. Wright, put his right hand to his forehead, stood tall and gave a military salute. He said "Sergeant Major Sir, I will be back in hour to pick you up".

He ran past us in the waiting room, jumped in his vehicle and was gone. Ten minutes later he returned. As he pulled up, I put my magazine down to watch. The driver again jumped out and ran to the side of his van. He opened the doors with care and helped out an elderly woman in her wheelchair. She looked to be about 101 years old. She was dressed in a neat floral dress, hat on her head, her gloved hands clutching her purse on her lap. All dressed up for her doctor's appointment.

The driver laughed and chatted with her as he wheeled her past the waiting area. Once again he approached the receptionist and announced with respect in his voice, "Excuse me, Mrs. Beachwood is here for her appointment". He treated his passenger as if royalty had arrived. He got down on one knee, knelt beside her wheelchair and took her frail gloved hand in his. He kissed her hand and said "Gorgeous, I'll be back in an hour to pick you up".

He ran past us again and left her sitting in her chair beaming. All I could think of as he climbed back in his driver's seat was that this was someone who obviously makes a choice to find the positives in what he chooses to do for a living.

He must understand that for many of his customers he may be one of the few people they see in a week. For some he may be like family. For Mr. Wright and Mrs. Beachwood, he makes a choice to brighten their day. If he dragged himself to work only seeing the 10%, how would that affect his attitude towards what he does and the very special people he serves?

I am sure his job is not perfect, without 10%s. I am sure some days he does not feel like picking people up and I am sure not all of his customers are as friendly as Mr. Wright and Mrs. Beachwood. He makes a choice. His choice is that he will stay focused on the positive 90%. The difference he makes.

− • −

Make a 90% list of why you wanted the job in the first place. Make a 10% list. If your 10% outweighs your 90% list, is it time to move on?

− • −

I can't just quit!

Some of you are reading this and saying, "I can't just quit my job!" I understand that. If that is your situation, is there some way you can make going to work more enjoyable?

If you have been venting about the same problems at work for more than three times, maybe it is time to lay that sucker out and ask yourself what you can control and what you can't. I will often do a workshop in my presentations where I will have the group lay out their 10%s on flip chart pages. Once all of them are written down we go back and look at the list. We circle which of their complaints they have control over and which they don't. Workshop after workshop so many people circle things that they just can't control. In the end there is only one or two concerns that they have direct control over. So my next question is, "What are you going to do about it"? If you can't control it, why complain about it? If you can, why not do something about it.

Maybe there is 90%s in the job that you have forgotten about. What if you approached the job with the attitude that if it's not time to leave, there must be something the job still has to teach you? Find out what that is. Maybe just trying to be grateful for your job will help you see it as a positive. Being employed is a blessing in itself.

The author Amy Tan said: *"If you can't change your fate, change your attitude"*

Maybe it's time to do just that.

– • –

Sometimes we stay in a job that slowly wears away at us. One time after a presentation I had a woman tell me "My job hurts my soul". I told her she had to leave. No job is worth your stress, your peace of mind, your family and certainly not your soul.

– • –

Here I go again on my own ...

No job I have ever had has been 100% perfect. They all have their 10%s.

My first job was working for my Dad in his Volkswagen repair shop in the back yard of our home. It was not an easy job, scrubbing parts, changing oil, setting valves on the Beetles. One of the 90%s were the long talks Dad and I would have around the work bench.

Years later I went to work as a bus girl in a restaurant and then worked in the retail industry in high school. I often say in my presentations we should all have to wait tables or work retail at least once in our lives for a reality lesson!

When I was 18 years old I packed up my 1965 Volkswagen Beetle (rebuilt by Dad and I) and I headed off down the highway and I popped in my "Whitesnake" cassette tape.

I arrived in a new city to live in my Aunt Susan's basement while I looked for a summer job. My aunt - my Dad's baby sister — is a very special lady in my life. Looking back I am so grateful for her opening her toddler- filled home to me. She gave me a great start, a safe place to start out on my own. She is still someone who opens her door when I need her.

I opened the classified ads and saw an ad that read "Tuxedo company looking for a young insightful person for their tuxedo sales department ". I am sitting at my Aunt's table thinking, I am 18 years old and I could get to measure men all day! Sign me up - it sounded like the job for me. Ha ha!

The job was not all about measuring men. It was very hard work. Scrubbing dirty rental shoes, picking through piles of BO-smelling tuxedos. Digging in the pockets of dirty tuxedos hoping you wouldn't find anything you didn't want to!! Ironing, altering, fitting and working in a very hot dry-cleaning plant. Plus the emotions of wedding couples who wanted their day to be perfect.

There were many 10%s but I loved the job and the people I worked with. I loved being a part of the wedding day of my customers. The 90%s outweighed the hard work and working conditions.

Then I was 24 years old and I had invested the first six years of my adult life in what I thought would be a summer job. I was very blessed to be mentored by some incredible people who helped to shape me as an entrepreneur.

I'll never forget arriving at work one hot summer morning to see a beautiful black Jaguar parked in my parking spot. Walking into the store I met a serious looking fellow in a blue suit in a heated discussion with the owners. The tuxedo company was going into receivership, on its way to bankruptcy. The man who drove the Jaguar was the receiver delivering the news. As strange as all this was, this ended up being a turning point in my life. I had always felt that if I got the chance there was some big changes I would make in this store. Four male co-workers and I sat in a coffee shop down the street and bounced some ideas around. We felt like we could do it and we took the chance. About a month later we were the new owners.

My partners stayed to run the original store and I moved to a branch store 550 kilometers away. New store for me. New city. New life. I packed up my K-Car with everything the bank didn't own and moved again. For old times' sake I popped in my "Whitesnake" cassette tape. "Here I go again on my own … "

I learned very quickly in my new store that having a great attitude would help me run my own business. There were many 10%s as I built up the business, but the greatest gift I could give my clients and, most importantly, my staff, was someone positive to work with. I made lots of mistakes but I persevered and I had the honor of working with the most amazing staff.

There was a bit of a buzz about this "young woman" who had come to town. Opening a tuxedo rental shop at 24 years of age was not what most young women did. I received a lot of media coverage and loved the opportunity to be interviewed and talk on camera. I was not shy and of course - I loved to talk!

One day, I was in my bank and the manager called me into his office. Ed was a kind man who always took the time to say hello and look you right in the eye. He asked me a question that would change the direction of my life. "I want you to speak at our next staff meeting and tell my staff what you do to stay positive. Can you do that?"

I said "Yes, I would love to". Then I remember leaving his office and feeling like I would throw up. I spent three weeks agonizing over the message then it hit me. How *did* I stay positive? I just kept focused on the positive 90%s.

Thirteen years ago, I stood in front of Ed's staff and shared my message about "Focusing on the Positive 90% instead of the 10%". A man who worked at the bank called me to say his wife and her staff would love to hear me too. Well as they say ... "The rest is history". I began to speak occasionally when people would call me, but I was still running my tuxedo store full time.

A few months later another opportunity appeared. I was planning my wedding to Darren, and in planning my own wedding I noticed that there was not enough Bridal Shows for the size of city we lived in. There seemed to be an opening for another Bridal Show - a wedding trade show where brides could go and visit wedding-related booths and see a fashion show. That year Darren and I organized, produced and promoted our first ever "Most Incredible Bridal Show".

Now I was juggling the demands of an ever-growing tuxedo store, a budding speaking career and an annual Bridal Show. I was receiving numerous awards for my entrepreneurial accomplishments, and beginning to study my path very carefully. What would have happened had I not taken the chances I had?

I was now 31 years old, running three successful businesses and I was pregnant. I had to make a choice. I knew that I wanted to be home for my children and I also knew I could not do everything.

I decided after 12½ years in the tuxedo industry, I was done. I needed to be done, I was getting burned out and was honestly tired of it and it was starting to show to my staff. I knew that I needed to practice what I preached to my audience members. If your negative 10% list outweighs your positive 90% list, it is time to move on. And my time had come. I sold my shares to my partners, and that chapter of my life was closed.

I was ready to start my new life as a full time speaker, tradeshow promoter and Mom. I set up my home office and adjusted to working alone after so many years in a busy store. I kept chanting 90% ... 90% ... 90%.

My speaking career boomed. In 22 months we had two angels, Jayda and John, to add to our family. Darren took "paternity leave" from his job and we traveled like crazy as I delivered my presentations in those months. After John's birth, Darren made a decision to quit his "good government job" to stay home full time and support my career and our traveling life. (I still think he quit so he could golf all summer!)

So now I am a full time-speaker who travels with my family. I don't know if that conjures up glamorous images for any of you but the reality is not always easy. It has its 90%s, but it definitely has its 10%s too. I have traveled with sick children, sick husband, sick me. I have packed and unpacked more times than I can count. I have "acrobatically" nursed my children in a moving vehicle (you Moms will know what I am talking about!). We have dealt with rescheduled flights, cancelled flights, rerouted to cities we'd never heard of. You name it and we have likely been there, intentionally or accidentally! But the 90%s are many. We have not missed a day with our children and we have albums of pictures filled with the "adventures" we have been on. We have had many 90% adventures but of course we have had a few 10%s too … and they've been just as memorable!

Snow in May?

We are traveling in the prairies on May 12th. Jayda is three years old and John is one. We pack up the van as we have done so many times, portable DVD in place, snacks, crafts, toys, work materials, suit, cooler, strollers, suitcases, laptop ... Whew ... off we go!

Heading down the highway we start to get a few snowflakes. Snowflakes in May? If you are from the prairies you know how to drive in bad weather, so we forge on. The weather gets worse and worse. May 12th! The next morning I am speaking to 250 people 550 miles away! This is not good!

We pull over in a small town of 2300 people to "let the storm pass" – only to discover that they have closed the highway in front of us. We get the last hotel room in town and it is definitely a 10%! The sign on the hotel room wall reads: "Do not let your hunting dogs on the beds".

With two very busy toddlers, we need to burn off some of their energy so we head out to into the snow-covered town. There is nothing to do so we spend four hours at the local clothing store trying on everything they have in the store, and another two hours at the Pharmasave looking at magazines and children's books.

We spend long meals in a restaurant and attempt to make our room a fun zone. We made forts with the blankets and chairs in the room. What else are you going to do with toddlers in a snow storm?

I never did make it to the presentation the next day. I phoned my client and explained the situation, with apologies. When they opened the highway, we turned around and came home. When my friends and family asked, "How was your trip?", I said the same thing I always say. "It was awesome."

When you look for the positive 90%s, they are there. When do I get to spend hours in a day just playing with my children in stores and blanket forts? When do I get to try on clothes for four hours? We ate the greatest home cooked-meals – that I didn't have to cook! - and I discovered later that close to 300 people had to "camp out" in the church basement. Hey at least we had a bed! We were safe, fed and able to get back home. Why complain about it?

– • –

Tommy Lasorda once said:

"Don't complain about your problems: 80% of people who hear them don't care. And the other 20% are glad you're having trouble".

Ha Ha, Mr. Lasorda ... I agree!

– • –

Viva Las Vegas

I was invited to speak in Las Vegas and I surprised Darren by inviting him along for the trip to celebrate our 10th Anniversary. Grandpa and Grandma came to stay with our angels for our first weekend away together since the children had been born. A second honeymoon!

For the first time in five years my husband and I sat on an airplane with no children! We arrived in our connecting city to discover that our flight was cancelled due to bad weather and the flights were backed up. I was to speak the next day in Las Vegas and this one, I could not miss. The clerk at the check-in counter informed us that we should go over to ticketing and see if there was anything they could do for us. He yelled "Good luck" as we bolted away.

I switched on my "positive attitude", and as we made our way up the line to the exhausted ticket agent, I started with," This must be a terrible day for you". With a deep sigh he said "Yes". I joked with him as I explained our predicament. After pounding away on his keyboard for what seemed to be hours he looked up and said," I think I found you two standby seats on a connecting flight to another city. Since the seats are standby, I can't guarantee you'll get on the flight. But if you make it, I was able to get you two seats from that city to Las Vegas. Oh, and one other thing, the flight has already began boarding and its gate is on the other side of the airport. As we dashed off, he yelled after us, "Don't worry. Your luggage will be rerouted".

We were like participants on the television show "The Amazing Race" as we raced to the gate. We waited breathlessly until the last two standby seats were called, they were ours, we made it! Whew, only one more city to go and we would be in Las Vegas.

We arrived in our next city and again ran as fast as we could to the next gate. We just made it. This time we were on our way to Las Vegas.

We arrived in Las Vegas at 7:00 pm, six hours behind schedule. Guess what? ... no luggage. No ticket agent to be found ... no one in the "lost luggage" office. We were tired and hungry so we headed to our hotel. The concierge at the hotel advises, "You'd better go buy something. The luggage is not usually found". I take her advice since I am the farthest thing from a natural beauty and I need "stuff" to get ready for my presentation the next morning.

Things keep getting stranger and stranger. Our room number was 911. Our buffet ticket was 666. It was 8:50 pm when we arrived at the mall. I had always heard that Vegas never sleeps, but I never imagined the mall would close at 9:00 pm! We had 10 minutes to shop. Darren and I headed in opposite directions and threw together an outfit that was two sizes too big. No time to find all the beauty aids I need!

Back at the hotel, I borrowed a curling iron from the woman working the front desk, I washed my face with the soap Darren showered with, and I rubbed hand cream on my face. So much for my "beauty routine".

I woke the next morning to discover the hotel's hot water heater had broken down. I showered in ice cold water and I delivered my presentation with a smile on my face and a safety pin digging me in the back. When I finished my engagement, Darren and I played the slot machines for hours — we figured our luck had to change! We didn't actually win any money but we had a great time.

Las Vegas has this great above-ground subway that you can ride on and see the entire strip. We decided to go for a ride to cap off our final night in Vegas.

At the first stop Darren jumped off to grab some bottled water from a vending machine. He said "I'll be quick". As he was watching the water drop down the machine, I was watching the subway doors close. I lunged towards the doors and just missed as they shut.

We were now looking at each other on opposite sides of the glass as the tram took off. My first instinct was to get off at the next stop and wait. Sounds logical doesn't it? Not to Darren. He decided it made more sense to wait where he was for me to come back.

So I am standing in a Las Vegas tram station at 11:00 pm on a Saturday night and I am in the company of some scary looking people. I am fearing for my life. As the train pulls up, I think well, Darren must be waiting at the first stop so I decide to get on the tram heading the other direction. As you might imagine, Darren has now decided to ride forward to find me!

To make a long story short over an hour later we finally connected at the same station. It felt like three hours. Let's just say I was not "focusing on the 90%" when I we finally connected! And the honeymoon was definitely over!

We were flying home the next morning. We arrived in our connecting city to discover that the gate number on our ticket was wrong. We were again ... running ... through a huge international airport.

When people asked about our trip, my answer was – you guessed it! – "It was awesome!"

We didn't become millionaires on the slot machines in Vegas, but we did make it safely to an engagement I needed to be at. I lived through the train station episode. We were particularly grateful when we contemplated what it would have been like to be running through airports with the children in tow!

If I had come home from Las Vegas and complained to my friends who had been sitting in two feet of snow, they would not have cared. I was in Vegas, they were in snow!! Now, I have great loving friends — and I mean that as nicely as I can make it sound —but ... they really don't care! We often complain about the 10%s of our jobs to people who have their own job 10%s too and shouldn't have to care about ours.

– • –

I love my job and I make a choice to be happy in a job that I choose to do. I am always amazed when I meet people who seem to feel it's necessary to justify that they enjoy what they do.

I meet people who say things like "Don't think I'm nuts but I love my job" or "As crazy as it sounds, I ACTUALLY really enjoy what I do". Why should it be so strange to enjoy what you choose to do?

– • –

3 years, 4 hours, 1 minute and 2 seconds left.

I worked with a group of people who were suffering from low moral issues. The second person to arrive at the training session was a man who was clearly unhappy about having to be there.

The blank name tags were to be filled out with the attendees' first name. As I watched the group preparing I noticed that this particular man had written on his tag. 3 years, 4 hours, 1 minute and 2 seconds left.

Now I know that most of us count days to retirement for a variety of reasons but this gentleman's name tag went with his attitude. As I looked at that tag, I thought that it must be difficult to work with someone who is just biding their time.

When people tell me that it is our youth today who are struggling with work ethic issues, I challenge that belief by asking, "Who is teaching them? Who do they get to learn from?"

Often today's young people are placed in organizations where they work beside (or work for) people who are just counting the days that they will have left until retirement. Young people tend to start their jobs with enthusiasm and they get placed next to people who do not want to be there anymore. So it is not surprising what attitudes they are absorbing as they sit beside people like that all day.

We have a choice to leave a legacy. What impression will you leave?

I am known as an optimist (well at least 90% of the time), which annoys a certain percentage of people. (Maybe 10%??) I know the ripple effect that my attitude has and I make a choice to be positive. That's called optimism. It is not easy being positive as you are not always "appreciated".

When people say to me, as they sometimes do, "I hate working with him, he is just too happy". I say back to them, "Who would you rather work with, him, or someone who drags himself to work every day and is an unhappy grouch?"

What are you known as at work? Are you a 90%'er or a 10%'er? An optimist or a grouch?

– • –

I will add that the youth need to reach out to the employees who have "been there a while" too. You can learn a lot from people. Some people in your workplace have a great deal of knowledge to share. All you need to do is ask.

– • –

Focus on the 90%

Co-workers ... and others around you

– • –

Raise your hand if you think a negative person can bring down a group?

When I ask this question during a presentation, most of the hands will fly in the air. Most people can share their own story of "one or two" that they work with ... or have worked with ... who have affected them in a negative way.

I have done a lot of my own research on what it is that affects people and their happiness in the workplace. I've been amazed by the number of people I met who started their job with their magnifying glass on the 90%s. They couldn't wait to get that job.

Then I would meet those same people a year later and they had changed. Now their magnifying glass had been moved to the negative 10%. What happened? Most say that one of the greatest feelings that affects them and their ability to stay focused on the positive 90% is "the other people that I work with".

They start positive, but soon say it is the people, not the job, that affect how they feel about going to work each day. They say that one negative person can bring down an entire department or organization. People often tell me they leave people, not their jobs.

I know in my own businesses that one or two negative employees can affect the morale of the entire group. So when clients would call me to speak and they would express concerns about morale, I wondered if they were dealing with the same issue. Could there be one or two in their group that were "affecting" the rest?

– • –

Bonnie and Tom

Early in my career a client invited me to deliver my attitude topic to his group of 40 employees. He explained that his branch was having issues with service delivery and low morale.

Days later I arrived for the engagement and the manager met me outside the training room door. He explained that before I went into the room he should warn me that he had a couple of employees who were causing some low morale issues. He explained to me how these two, Bonnie and Tom might not treat me properly as a speaker and I should be prepared. I asked the manager not to point out who these two were because I can usually tell. I reassured him that I was ready and he kind of pushed me into the room wishing me a "good luck".

This was an evening event outside of regular work hours and the staff were "strongly recommended to attend". Let's just say, that is not a warm and fuzzy room of people to stand in front of! I had to enter in the back door, which was in the middle of the back wall. I had to then walk behind all the staff in the back row and up the side to the front. The staff were all seated at tables facing forward, waiting as I was being introduced.

As I walked past the back table to make my way to the front, a woman announced as I walked by, so loudly that the entire room could hear, *"What does she weigh, like 80 pounds?!"* She caught me off guard and I looked her way. (Have you ever noticed that women can often be extremely judgmental of each other?) Each of my audience members receives a mini-magnifying glass to remind them of my message and on the back of that magnifying glass is my picture. I looked down at the table in front of the outspoken woman and saw that she had doodled on that picture – on my face! She blacked out my front teeth, drew a long goatee on my chin and big devil horns coming out of my forehead! I noticed her name tag ... it was Bonnie. The man sitting next to her was - no surprise, Tom.

While I was up front delivering my presentation, Bonnie and Tom ... visited. They laughed and carried on like I was not even in the room. Bonnie blew big bubbles with her gum. They were very disrespectful to me and everyone else in the room who was trying to listen. You could feel the tension in the room and I could tell the effect they had on the others.

What amazed me was that obviously these two had already decided before I even arrived what they thought of me and the training evening. Long before I arrived they had their magnifying glasses on the 10%. The second thing that amazed me was how this pair was acting in front of their boss!

During the break two separate women came to me with tears in their eyes, telling me how they were affected by these two and their negative attitudes. One person said to me *"Do you see how they are treating you, a stranger? Imagine how they treat us"*. Good point. The next person took me out into the hall and said that the stress she feels at work is affecting her marriage because she takes this home with her at the end of the day.

When we regrouped after the break I asked the question I often ask my audience members in my sessions. "Do you believe a negative person can bring down a group?" Guess who put her hand up first? Bonnie. I am standing up front thinking...she is part of the problem and she doesn't even know she is a problem. She can't even see her own negative attitude.

I went on in that session to explain how people's negative individual's attitudes at work can have a profound effect on the entire group. I hoped that Bonnie and Tom heard me that night. I hoped that they would drive home and think about how they could improve. It was a pivotal night for me because it was one of the first times I had met a group that admitted it was negative individual coworkers that were affecting the performance and morale of the group. Most don't see the connection. Most don't realize the "ripple effect" as shared in the job chapter of this book.

– • –

So what do we do with the Bonnies and Toms in our work places? I used to say to my own staff, as I have said to many audiences ... "Don't worry about them. Focus on the 90% of the people who are in a good mood and want to be at work". I used to tell my own staff to just ignore them and hang out with the people who do have their magnifying glass on the 90%s.

As a manager of people, it was my responsibility to deal with an employee's negative attitude before it affected everyone else - but I often tried to ignore it. I was honestly too busy. So when my employees came into my office to vent their concerns about fellow coworkers my advice was … just stay away from them. Stay focused on the people who do enjoy their job.

But … isn't that easier said than done?

Early in my career as a speaker I also stood up in front of audiences offering them the same advice on dealing with their negative coworkers — it didn't seem enough. Ignoring those negative individuals was not that easy. I prayed over what to tell these groups and then God presented a gift, a gift with the name … Diane.

— • —

The "B"

I arrived for a presentation that would be attended by 100 people. We would spend the entire day together and we would share a morning session on focusing on the positive 90% of your job and your coworkers. In the afternoon we would "switch gears" and focus on themselves as individuals and their family life.

Before I arrived, I found out from one of the managers that they had an employee in their group they called "The B". What concerned me was that the leader of this group of people was calling her employee this horrible name.

As I began to set things out to prepare for my presentation a continual stream of people came up to me at the front of the room, saying things to me like … *"Has anyone told you yet?"… "Has anyone warned you about "The B"?*

One by one, they told me stories about this woman coming in to work in the morning and going straight into her office without saying good morning or making eye contact with anyone. She stays in her office all day — hardly never comes out for "coffee

time" and never attends the special lunches the social committee arranges. As one woman explained with disgust in her voice, "And the worst part is, she never comes to the Christmas party".
It was clear there was a great deal of energy spent on this woman and her behavior. There would be no name tags at this event and I had learned that "The B's" name was in fact, Diane. I wondered if I would be able to pick Diane out. I can really read people's energies and sad, unhappy people are usually easy to find …

As the audience filled the room, everyone sat together in groups, with the exception of one woman, who chose to sit at the back corner of the room by herself. My guess was, I had found Diane.

I shared my morning message focused on the work portion of our life. I talked about focusing on the positive 90% of our jobs and how important the ripple effect is. I then shared my message about co-workers and how we all work with "one or two" difficult people. I went on to share what I had shared with audiences many times before …

"Don't worry about them, focus on the 90% you do

enjoy working with and ignore the 10% who are a pain".

I wrapped up the morning session and it was now time for lunch. We all piled into the cafeteria and again ... 99 people sat among their friends and Diane sat alone. It was as if there was an imaginary protective shield around her that was keeping people away from her - and my guess was, it kept her from having to deal with others too. Now as I watched Diane sitting alone, God called me to go and sit with her. I figured I had nothing to lose; I do not have any agenda with how she has treated me and don't have to work with her for the next 20 years. Besides ... she is research for me!

I took a deep breath and walked with my tray full of food to her table. As she looked down eating her meal I asked the top of her head, "May I sit and eat with you?" With one swift move she kicked the chair across from her and said, "It is a free country, do what you want". I was a little afraid but I had come this far!

It was obvious this woman was hurting. So searching for something to say I said, *"My name is Darci"*. She looked up from her meal, looked me right in the face and said point blank, *"Stop"*. She went on to say, *"The thing I do not like about this morning's session is that you just gave my 99 colleagues permission to continue not caring about me."*

I was taken a back and my pride was hurt, but I have a thick hide and I am always interested in improving myself. I want my message to have an impact so I asked her, *"How did I do that?"* I moved to the chair next to her so I could let her speak quietly.

So for the next 45 minutes Diane completely altered my thinking about the 10%s we work with and know in our lives. She completely changed how I view the Bonnies, the Toms ... and the Dianes ... of the world.

Here is what she shared. She started out by saying, *"Well I know what they call me here ... and it hurts. There is nothing worse than being gossiped about when they do not know my story.*

You know Darci, I have worked here for three years and no one has ever given me the time of day. I am not saying that I am an approachable person but you would think that in three years someone would at least reach out a bit. Maybe I deserve to be treated this way but I honestly do not know how else to act right now. I act this way because I am barely coping with my life. My personal life is hell. Let me tell you about my life Darci and maybe it will shed some light on why some of the "10%'ers" — as you call them — act the way they do.

I wake up in the morning next to a man who has been passed out drunk for years. My husband lost his job due to his alcoholism and I had to get this job. I am the breadwinner for our family now. If that isn't stressful enough — I walk down the hall to my 17 year old daughters bedroom … my little girls room … and stand outside that door before I open it. You see, my daughter has gotten in with the wrong crowd. Sometimes I open that door and my daughter is not in there. I spend my morning making calls trying to track my girl down. Some days I go to work still wondering where she is. Some days I feel like I am barely coping with my day and it is only 7:30am! I put my suit on, I put my lipstick on, I look myself in the mirror and I say to myself, Diane, you can do this one more day.

I arrive at work and I rush into my office and … hide. Work is the only place I do something … right. I don't come out for coffee because I don't have the energy to listen to everyone complain about their job. This is a great place to work. I don't come to the stupid lunches they put together because I am so sick of my coworkers complaining about their petty lives and their petty problems when my life is so full of problems.

She looked at me and with tears streaming down her face she said to me — "And Darci, how am I supposed to take HIM to the Christmas party?"

I am a crier so we are now both crying. I am a hugger too. I love to hug people…especially those who are not huggers — it is like hugging a piece of plywood!

I took a chance and reached over and hugged Diane. I figured, maybe it had been a long time since she had one. As I pulled away from her I noticed something ... her shield was down.

I went back in front of this group for my afternoon session and here is what I said:

"I would like to add something to this morning's session. You know the 10%ers in our lives? What if we viewed them through our 90% magnifying glass rather than through our 10% glass? What if when we saw

another person we chose to see the positives in them first?

Would it change a "culture"? Would it create more "team atmosphere'?

No one in this room is perfect. We all have our faults, we all have our stresses and we all have ... a story. What if we cut each other a bit more slack and tried to view each other in a more positive light? What if we recognize the fact that we may not know what is going on in some people's lives that may be causing them to act the way they do? What if we remember that work is the happiest place some people go in their lives. What if we take the time to care and have compassion and empathy for another human being?"

The manager emailed me the next day saying they heard my message loud and clear and they would work on their kindness to Diane. I prayed they did. I also prayed that Diane would get the help that she, her husband and their daughter needed.

– • –

Think for a minute who are your Bonnies, Toms or Dianes? How can you view them differently?

– • –

Maybe it is you who is changing?

I told this story to a Christian group and after my presentation I received an email from a woman who told me that they too had a "Diane" within their group. She shared in her email that after my presentation the group started a prayer circle for their Sheila. Every time they caught themselves gossiping – a very non- Christian thing to do – they would say a prayer for Sheila instead. The woman who emailed me said; "It is so amazing Darci - after a month of praying for her we thought to ourselves ... wow ... Sheila is changing".

I emailed her back and said "Maybe you are the ones who are changing?"

When we change how we "view" others - we choose to see them in a more positive way. A 90% way.

The 90% View

Viewing people through my 90% magnifying glass has transformed how I manage and lead my team members. Viewing our employees through our positive 90% magnifying glass is a wonderful way to stay focused on building people up.

Self-esteem is a fragile thing and we as leaders are responsible, in part, for the self-esteem of our employees. We need to make choices to see the positives in our employees first.

Now when my employees come to me with concerns about a fellow employee I say to them - "I wonder what is going on in their life that is causing them to act this way". I then take responsibility for calling that employee into my closed office and asking them if they are in fact ... okay? Something amazing started to happen. They started to share. And I started to see the employee with more compassion and empathy. I have learned that work is the happiest place in some employee's lives. I now take my role in their happiness very seriously.

I remember that this person is someone's child. This person is someone's spouse or partner. They could be someone's Mom or Dad. When we change our reaction to people and how we view them, our attitude changes too.

Viewing people through the 90% magnifying glass has not only transformed the way I view people at work but the people outside of work as well. My step-mom Sandy laid a great foundation for me by showing me that everyone has a story. She is a kind woman who always sees the good in others. She taught me many things and she taught me that people are doing what they need to do to get by. People deal with depression, health issues, aging parents, divorces teenagers, debt, addictions ... the list goes on. People lead big lives. Everyone has a story. Some of the most unhappy people I have met on the outside are the ones who are going through the most on the inside.

When a cashier or waitress is rude I cut her some slack. How do I know how she is being treated at work or at home?

When a young person does not seem to know their job, I offer patience. I view them as someone else's child. How would I want someone to treat my own child in that situation?

There was a time where even in traffic I would get bent out of shape if someone cut me off. I now wonder, what is going on in their lives? When I was pregnant I used to drive and think, "What if my water breaks and that guy will not let me in to get to the hospital?". So now I view all drivers that way. What if the woman driving is pregnant and needs to get to the hospital? What if the man driving is going to meet his pregnant wife at the hospital? I let everyone in on that premise. I realize that pregnancy isn't likely the cause of all the rude driving I see on the road these days but the principle is the same. I try to cut everybody a little slack.

When I am in the car while Darren is driving, he lets everyone in with a wave — and he mutters to me with heavy sarcasm, "Ya ya I know, her water is breaking."

Have you never been late?
Have you never been rushed in the car?

I once heard a comedian say "When you are feeling frustrated behind an elderly person for driving slow … just imagine if they drove fast."

It changes how we see others if we see them in a positive 90% way.

– • –

My sister Amy once sent me a magnet that said:

Before you criticize another person you should walk a mile in their shoes, that way when you criticize them, you are a mile away ... and you have their shoes!

Ha ha.

– • –

Some of you reading are very positive people. Some of you are the ones who pump everyone else up at work. Kudos to you. Being positive is not easy. I know this firsthand. Working with or being with negative people when you are trying to stay positive is not easy either. Stay strong. You don't own it, you can only control you. Keep yourself positive so that you enter all interactions with others a full positive person.

So what if you still have to deal with unhappy people? No matter how hard you try to love, pray for and care about ... there will still be one or two people who choose to keep their shield up. Those who seem to "rock everyone's world", the ones who really do not think they are the ones with the problem. I have met them, I know them, I have worked with them, they have worked for me, I have prayed for them and I have tried to love them. Some of them continue to be rude and unhappy. What do we do with them?

I had a very close friend go through a very emotional weekend-long addiction recovery program with an addicted family member. One of the many things they learned that weekend was that they did not own the problem of the person with the addiction. This made a lot of sense to me. Not easy to do ... but it made sense. Only the person with the addiction owns that problem. I related that to the people who I can't seem to reach people with a negative attitude own that attitude. It is not yours. You can't change people, only your reaction to them.

Only you can control you. That's it. We can't control others and their behaviors. We have all tried. Some people like the shield they build around themselves and quite frankly, some people just want to be left alone.

– • –

What have you done to reach out to the "10%'s"?

– • –

We have to get along!

At a recent Association Conference, a group of employees from one office were having such a great time. The entire morning that I shared my message they were having the most fun. At the break I asked them, "How do you all get along so well?" A few around the table shared with excitement how they had all worked together for years and they loved working together. I shared with them that that is remarkable because sometimes people who work together all day sometimes lose the ... enthusiasm ... for each other.

One woman from the table stood up and said proudly ..."We live and work in a small community ... we have no choice ... we HAVE to get along!".

As I walked away I thought ... what a great attitude! Imagine if we implemented that within all groups? What if we decided we just HAVE to get along!

— • —

The greatest way to create teamwork is to have fun together. It is much easier with people who enjoy their job and come to work positive! Since you "have to" work together, how can we make it more enjoyable?

What if we started each morning with a positive 90%? What if we started each meeting with a positive 90%? What if we focused on the 90% of our clients that are happy?

— • —

Your clients

– • –

I don't think it is realistic to keep 100% of clients happy. In fact, I think it is impossible. I also think it is an unrealistic expectation we put on ourselves, and our staff. I think 90% is good enough. But don't we tend to focus on the 10% who will never be happy no matter what we do? We spend 90% of our time on those 10% of our clients, some of whom were probably never going to be happy in the first place.

– • –

The Accountability Agreement.

I spent the first few years of my life working as a manager not really sure how to manage. Most people are not trained for this position. I spent a lot of time focusing on the negative 10% of my staff. I would come in the morning and find what was not done, point out what they did not do well. I was not very much fun to work for. I was what Kenneth Blanchard in his book "One Minute Manager" calls a Seagull Manager. Someone who flies in, squawks at everyone and leaves.

If my staff were doing the best they could, what more could I ask of them? They were only 90%. No one was perfect, but again, neither was I.

I learned as the years went on that there were just a certain percentage of clients who were never going to be happy. We could have shoved $1000 bills in the pockets of their rental tuxedos and some of them would still have found something wrong.

I decided that if we really provide our customers with the best possible service we can, we should not feel stress. I really mean that. This led to the development of the "accountability agreement".

Here is how it would go. My half of the accountability agreement would be that I would promise each staff member that I would be the best Manager I could be for them. I would arrive with a smile, I would try my very best to focus on their positive 90%s and I would be the example of what I was asking them to be. Their half would be that they would be accountable to me and the business. I would ask them to promise me that they would give the best possible service they could to our clients with a positive attitude each day. Okay, almost each day. Our clients were expecting our best possible service for their wedding day and how they looked for that special day, was very important to them. I told them they should have very little stress in a very stressful job.

I always worked Mondays because that was the day the tuxedos were returned and the day you heard any complaints. Inevitably someone would return unhappy. It was a high variable business and many things could go wrong with a rented garment. Some days I could feel the spit hit my face as a customer yelled at me about his broken tuxedo pants and how they practically fell down while he was walking down the aisle. (Maybe you are a member of the "sworn at by your customer club" in your business too!). I would listen, empathize and do whatever was needed to fix the unfixable. If at any point of his yelling at me he said anything negative about a member of my staff I would politely say to him, "I trust my staff and I know they did the best they could.".

When the customer left, happy again— most of the time, I would ask my employee, "Did you give this customer the best possible service you could? Did you triple check the pant clips and the measurements?" She would always honestly answer yes. I would tell her then to go home that night and feel no stress.   If you give the best you possibly can what more can I ask of you? But the flipside was this … if any employee was honest with me that no they did not do the best they could, they could have done better ... those were the times they felt stress. When their part of the accountability agreement was not in place.

It has been a powerful tool in my manager's tool box. 90% is good enough.

– • –

Are you stressed about the customer service delivery in your job? Ask yourself, are you truly accountable?

– • –

Your comments are important to us.

In my busy speaking months I stay in a hotel, on average, once or twice a week. You know that little card in the room that says, "Your comments are important to us"? The one where the hotel asks you to please take the time to fill it out and let them know how they did?

Well, I have decided to take the time to do that as many times as I can. I have decided that I will take the time to fill that card out because I ask thousands of audience members a year to do the same for me. I ask them, how did I do? Since I am a positive person, I like to take the time to write the positives of my stay. Not only do I write a positive or two or even three, I take the time to find out the name of any staff member who impressed me with their service. I tape my business card to the comment card and tell them that I speak on attitude and customer service for a living and I think they did an exceptional job (if they did) and I tell them why we enjoyed our stay. You can find positive if you look for it. Even in the rooms that have "Don't clean your guns with the towels" posted in the bathroom.

I have now filled out dozens and dozens of those cards and I take the time to do this even though I don't really have time. I am sitting at the desk in the hotel room filling out the card while Darren is trying to get out the door with two, yes count them, two luggage carts filled to the top. We have work stuff, suitcases, toys, strollers, car seats, etc. Jayda and John are anxious to escape and run down the halls. Needless to say, Darren is not always supportive of me doing this in the midst of the chaos of getting out the door to catch our plane.

Why do I bother? Because I think it would be really nice for a hotel and its employees to hear something positive because people tend to crab on comment cards. I also know that some managers have not been to the Focus on the 90% seminar and do not share positives with their staff. It could be what an employee needed to hear. Why else? I am interested to see how many will respond to my positive comments.

Of the dozens of hotels we have stayed in year after year guess how many of them have responded to my glowing comments? If you were an optimist you would say 90% responded, right? Some of you would say 10%. In fact, in all my years of writing dozens and dozens of cards, I've received two replies.

Now filling the cards out has become a bit of a game to see how many will write me back!

When I tell this story in my workshops, many of my audience members tell me stories of times of when they have stayed a hotel and they had not been happy with the service and complained. They tell me stories of getting a free room upgrade or flowers or chocolates in the room. Some have told me about surprise packages full of toys for their kids to play with! Huh?? So is the message that if I had complained instead, I would have received free things for my family?

Many people say to me, "I bet you if you had written a complaint on those cards you would have heard back!" Sadly, they are probably right. But isn't that what we tend to do? Focus on the 10% of our customers who are not happy, rather than focusing on the 90% who are? The squeaky wheel gets the oil.

I think my family and I are great customers at a hotel. We have great kids, we always clean up after ourselves, we stay for long stays (often at the same hotel over and over again in one year). We need the biggest room, we use the overpriced telephone and internet services and we eat a lot in the restaurant! If I managed those hotels, I would want to thank us for saying nice things and invite us back. That is a lot of business!

I know we can learn a lot from our unhappy customers. We can learn great ways to improve our business but if we spend all our time on them, we forget about the ones that are already happy. If we do not make them feel appreciated, they will find someone else who does.

I have met people over the years who manage hotels and I have asked them, "Why am I not being responded to?" I have been told that when the pile of comment cards arrive on their desk on Monday mornings they pick through the pile and find the unhappy 10% comment cards first. By the time they finish putting out fires with the 10%s, they have no time left to deal with — and thank — the happy 90% comment cards like mine.

Sound familiar in your business? We spend so much time trying to make happy the unhappy customers that we often forget about the happy ones. No the

customer isn't always right – 10% of the time they
are just cranky.

– • –

*Take a good look at where you spend your energy: is it
on the 90% or the 10% of your customers? What can
you do to make your 90% customer feel appreciated
and wanting to come back?*

– • –

Itchy pants

During my time as manager of that tuxedo rental
shop, I rented tuxedos to tens of thousands of men.
Renting tuxedos was not an easy job but it was very
rewarding. In our busy peak season we would
average a few dozen customers a day. Most would be
happy. In a week there would always be one or two
who weren't. It was inevitable. No matter how hard
we tried, there was always that unhappy 10%. They
would be rude and disrespectful to me and my staff.
They would be rude and disrespectful to me in front
of their future brides, the brides' mother, her

bridesmaids and even his own mother! (Often the women in the prospective groom's life had a say in the tuxedo rental too!)

You know what I wanted to say to the bride who was about to marry Mr.10%er don't you? RUN!!!!!

Whenever they would leave the shop, my employees would always say: "Thank goodness we aren't marrying him!"

We weren't selling funeral plots: we were renting tuxedos! For the happiest day of their lives! For the gentlemen reading this — isn't your wedding day the happiest day you remember? (Just nod your head up and down!).

And who would my staff and I talk about on our very rare coffee break? Of course, the 10%! Not the dozens and dozens of happy customers. We had dozens of thank you cards and wedding pictures posted on the wall. We would get flowers, pies and chocolates as gifts. But we did not tend to think about that. Our focus always leaned towards the ones that we could not make happy.

I would get home at the end of a long retail day and when Darren would ask me how my day was, I would talk about the one or two. Not the dozens and dozens. Not the pie and chocolate!

I used to lie in bed at night and think about ways to get back at those 10% customers ... what if I made the crotch of his pants itchy for his wedding? ... (Just kidding!)

So I decided to do some research. I was beginning to get busy in my speaking career now, and I was always interested in people's moods. I decided to use my customers as research and here is what I gathered. The first thing that I gathered was - something that did not surprise me when dealing with this cranky groom - four out of five of his groomsmen- for the most part, his friends - were cranky too. People surround themselves with what they know. What did surprise me though was that about 90% of the time when his Dad would come in for his tuxedo fitting, his Dad would be rude to me too. The apple does not fall far from the tree. People act the way they are taught to act.

I started to realize how unrealistic it was to try and keep everyone happy. Some people are never going to be. I could probably have called the limousine company, the hotel the wedding was booked at and the florist and ask them if they had dealt with a particular 10% groom I was having trouble with. I'll bet you, they would have had a problem with him too.

Now don't get me wrong. We made mistakes: my gosh, we rented tuxedos!! That was just the makings for mistakes! I am talking about the people we were trying to do our best with ... and it just wasn't good enough. That taught me that some people are just never going to be happy.

– ● –

Think about the percentage of your customers who are happy with the service you provide. If you don't know, it is a great idea to ask. If the satisfaction rate is around 90%, you need to stop being so hard on yourself. Ask yourself, am I doing the best I can? If the answer is yes, lay your head down at night and sleep peacefully.

– ● –

When you didn't like my tuxedos and we had made a mistake it was tough on me because I really cared about my customers. I understood that your 10% was part of the business. When I became a speaker and an audience member didn't like me that was different. It felt more personal.

For thirteen years now, I have been speaking and training. For the first few years of my career, I didn't supply my audience with an evaluation form to share their comments on what they thought of me and my presentation. It was great. If you didn't like what I did ... you had nothing to write it on! Ha ha.

A few years into my career, I realized how important it was to gather feedback from both my client and my audience members. So I offered my first set of evaluation forms and I haven't looked back.

I have learned so much about how to improve my message ... and my delivery. I am committed to continual growth and learning. You have to really ask yourself sometimes, is there some truth in constructive and helpful criticism? It is impossible to be perfect but what can I constantly be learning?

– • –

Do you ever have those days? Where everything just goes ... great?

– • –

It's all about the hair

Let me tell you about one of the best presentations I have ever delivered. "I was invited to speak at a Women's Conference. I was the first speaker in a full day line-up of speakers. It was my job to "pump them up" and start the conference on a positive note. I arrived around 6:30 a.m. at the ballroom which was incredible. The sun was rising and pouring warm orange light into this ceiling-to-floor-windowed room. I had about an hour to myself in the room to prepare and I prayed that God would use me as he needed to that day. The sun was now streaming into this beautiful ballroom and dancing off the crystal chandelier. It was one of the most magical rooms I have been in and no one had even arrived yet.

At 8:00 a.m. the first of the 250 women started to arrive and the energy started to build. Pack 250 women in a room and you are bound to feel some great energy! This group had paid their own money to come together as women for a much needed women's day.

I deliver many presentations in a year and since I am not perfect I sometimes deliver presentations that do not go that well. Not that day. Everything worked that day. The audience was warm and inviting. During the "sharing" portion of my presentation I had women telling stories of overcoming cancer, losing children and many stories of how women had decided to be happy in their lives by focusing on their positive 90%s. It is always amazing to me that the people who have been through the most in their lives seem to rise above it all and live life to the fullest.

It was an emotional, meaningful morning. There were women hugging and crying. You could feel the estrogen pumping through that crowd!

The three hours together ended with a standing ovation and a long line of hugs from audience members. I knew that I had delivered a purposeful presentation that day. I was selling and signing books and CDs in a flurry of activity. I could hardly get out of the room! I felt like Tony Robbins!

When I arrived back to the hotel room Darren asked what he always does: "How did it go?". I replied, "It was one of the best presentations I have ever delivered". We packed up and flew home.

A couple of days later I got down to reading the 250 evaluation forms. Every single woman in that room took the time to fill one out. Women who did not want to share their story in front of the group, did so on their evaluation form. I read stories from so many women who overcame so much in their lives.

In addition to the evaluation forms, I had women emailing me, telling me what they did differently after they had heard my message. Managers who went back to their workplace and passed out my mini-magnifying glasses to their staff and started a 90% culture in their work places. Women who shared how they went home and slid that magnifying glass across the dinner table to their spouse and said, "I want us to find the positives in each other again". Mothers who realized they had not told their children enough how much they love them. Everyone truly did have a story. Powerful stuff. I knew I had touched many lives that day. I even had a husband email and say, "I don't know what you said to my wife but she is sure nice to me lately!"

I assumed that since it was such a meaningful presentation, the response that I received from the women in the audience would be positive. And it was. I received 249 heartfelt evaluation forms and countless emails from women who shared their life stories with me. Positive, glowing comments about what they were going to do differently in their lives after hearing my 90% message.

At the bottom of the pile I had one evaluation left to read. I assumed it would be as positive as the others were. But what I read was, "You sucked and your hair is too big".

I sat back in my chair, totally stunned. I felt sick to my stomach. Sucked? No I didn't! Sometimes I am not as good as I could have been but … sucked??? Who would write something like that? And more to the point: Did I deserve it?

I sat in my chair trying to visualize in my mind all of the shorthaired women in the room. Why? I figured that no big-haired woman would say this to another big hair!

At that moment Darren walked in the office and could tell I was upset. I explained to him that the "best presentation I every delivered" was not so great after all. When he asked why, I handed him the evaluation to read.

After reading it, he fell on the ground laughing. He laughed on the floor for five minutes. When he regained his composure, he asked me what the other 249 said. I told him how great they were.

Then he said, "You are upset about this one evaluation and you have 249 positive ones sitting in front of you? You know the difference you made yesterday. Practice what you preach Hon. You tell other people that 10% aren't going to be happy not matter what. One out of 250 is a lot less than 10%, so you're ahead of your own predictions. Besides ... you probably look like her ex-husband's new wife". And he walked out of the office.

I sat there smiling, thinking, "Good point Darren.". Besides, I am a girl from the 1980s and damn proud of my big hair!

I am what I am and I have learned that I have to practice my own message. My life is speeding by and I need to make sure all of the 10%s in my life are kept in perspective. My life is full of 90%s. That is where I choose to keep my focus.

Focus on the 90%

Epilogue

So my reader friend, we've had a great journey together. I hope that I've delivered that other tool that I offered you for your life's tool box.

Take care of you first. Love yourself. Love your 90%s. You are not perfect. Forgive yourself. I don't know what % of your life you have lived yet but do what you need to do to feel better and live life to the fullest because you never know which day may be your last. Do not waste another one.

Love your family. Give them your greatest 90%s. My grandpa used to say "There will not be a U-haul behind your hearse". You can't take what you bought with you. Only the love of the people in your families. Do not live one more day with guilt. Give the best of you to the people who matter the most.

Go back to your work and make a choice to focus more on the 90% positive. Life is too short to drag yourself to work everyday. Leave a legacy. Be remembered as someone who came to work and made the best of it. Be grateful to be employed.

Look at the people around you with a new perspective. People do have the ability to affect us but let's rise above that and choose to be positive. View people through your 90% magnifying glass. Everyone is dealing with their own 10%s. Choose to be a positive person with others. Let's live our lives so that our funeral is full of people whom we have touched.

God Bless.

Focus on the 90%

Meet Darci Lang

Darci is one of the most popular and proficient professional speakers in Canada. In her fourteen year career as a motivator and trainer, she has been invited to speak to numerous government departments, conferences, staff functions and development days across the continent. She shares an easy-to-apply message that everyone can relate to. The message is simple; you have a choice when it comes to your attitude, professionally and personally. The choices you make affect yourself and your team.

A positive attitude is the foundation of Darci's success. She has owned and operated three separate companies, and managed a diverse and varied range of employees. As the present owner of X-L Enterprises and previous owner of award-winning Mallabar Tuxedo Rentals in Regina, Darci understands that working effectively within an area or unit requires you to work on yourself first.

Business people who observed Darci's success as an entrepreneur and manager, began to ask her to share her personal story about shaping successful businesses. As the demand increased, she launched her third business endeavor, as a professional speaker and traincr, sharing her message about "Focusing on the 90%".

Her dedication and entrepreneurial skill have paid off. Darci receives rave reviews from clients and audiences wherever she appears. She has also won the Saskatchewan Woman Entrepreneur of the Year Award and an Achieving Business Excellence (ABEX) Award. She was a finalist for the Canadian Woman of the Year Award and a three-time nominee for the nationally recognized Entrepreneur and Young Entrepreneur of the Year Awards.

She is truly someone who walks the talk — while balancing her life at the same time. Darci's home in Regina, with husband and business partner Darren and their two children, demonstrates clearly that Focusing on the 90% applies to family fun and values as well as the business and professional arena.

Focus on the 90%

Focus on the 90%

Focus on the 90%

Focus on the 90%

Focus on the 90%

Focus on the 90%

DARCI LANG
Focus on the 90%

Order Form

Item	Per Unit Price	Number	Total required
Darci Lang "Focus on the 90% One simple tool to change the way you view your life.	$20		
Darci Lang "Focus on the 90%" Live CD	$20		
CD & Book Set	$30		
Sub Total			
GST (5% of Sub Total)			
PST (5% of Sub Total, Saskatchewan residents only)			
Shipping and Handling ($3 for each Book or CD; $6 for each Book/CD Set)			
		Order Total	

Order and Payment Options

Order Option

Payment Option

Mail to:
XL Enterprises
P.O. Box 32077
Regina, SK
S4N 6E0
or
Fax to:
(306) 569-1356

❏ Cheque or money order (payable to XL Enterprises)

❏ Visa
   Cardholder name: _____
   Card #: _____
   Expiry Date: _____

❏ MasterCard
   Cardholder name: _____
   Card #: _____
   Expiry Date: _____

Delivery Information

Name: _____ Phone (____) _____

Address: _____

City: _____ Prov./State: _____ Postal/Zip: _____

Ph: (306) 569-1354   Fax: (306) 569-1356   E-mail: info@darcilang.com
www.darcilang.com

Focus on the 90%